Abraham Kuyper

Calvinism

Six Lectures Delivered in the Theological Seminary at Princeton

Abraham Kuyper

Calvinism
Six Lectures Delivered in the Theological Seminary at Princeton

ISBN/EAN: 9783337170493

Printed in Europe, USA, Canada, Australia, Japan

Cover: Foto ©Lupo / pixelio.de

More available books at **www.hansebooks.com**

The L. P. Stone Lectures for 1898-1899

CALVINISM

Six Lectures Delivered in the Theological Seminary at Princeton

BY

ABRAHAM KUYPER, D.D., LL.D., M.P.

Professor in the Free University, Amsterdam
Member of the States General of Holland

NEW YORK   CHICAGO   TORONTO

Fleming H. Revell Company

Publishers of Evangelical Literature

INDEX.

FIRST LECTURE.

CALVINISM A LIFE SYSTEM.

A traveller from the old European Continent, disembarking on the shore of this New World, feels as the Psalmist says, that "his thoughts crowd upon him like a multitude". Compared with the eddying waters of your new stream of life, the old stream in which he was moving seems almost frostbound and dull; and here, on American ground, for the first time, he realizes how so many divine potencies, which were hidden away in the bosom of mankind from our very creation, but which our old world was incapable of developing, are now beginning to disclose their inward splendour, thus promising a still richer store of surprises for the Future.

You would not, however, ask me to forget the superiority which, in many respects, the Old World may still claim, in your eyes, as well as in mine. Old Europe remains even now the bearer of a longer historical past, and .therefore stands before us as a tree rooted more deeply, hiding between its leaves some more matured fruits of life. You are yet in your Springtide,—we are passing

through our Fall; — and has not the harvest of Autumn
an enchantment of its own?

But, though, on the other hand, I fully acknowledge
the advantage you possess in the fact, that (to use another
simile) the train of life travels with you so immeasureably
faster than with us,—leaving us miles and miles behind,—still we both feel that the life in Old Europe is
not some thing separate from life here; it is one and
the same current of human existence that flows through
both Continents.

By virtue of our common origin, *you* may call us bone
of your bone,—*we* feel that you are flesh of our flesh,
and although you are outstripping us in the most discouraging way, you will never forget that the historic cradle
of your wondrous youth stood in our old Europe, and
was most gently rocked in my once mighty Fatherland.

Moreover, besides this common parentage, there is
another factor which, in the face of even a wider
difference, would continue to unite your interests and
ours. Far more precious to us than even the development of human life, is the crown which ennobles it,
and this noble crown of life for you and for me rests
in the Christian name. That crown is our common
heritage. It was not from Greece or Rome that the
regeneration of human life came forth;—that mighty
metamorphosis dates from Bethlehem and Golgotha;
and if the Reformation, in a still more special sense,
claims the love of our hearts, it is because it has
dispelled the clouds of sacerdotalism, and has unveiled
again to fullest view the glories of the Cross. But, in
deadly opposition to this Christian element, against the

very Christian name, and against its salutiferous influence in every sphere of life, the storm of Modernism has now arisen with violent intensity.

In 1789 the turning point was reached.

Voltaire's mad cry, "Down with the scoundrel" was aimed at Christ himself, but this cry was merely the expression of the most hidden thought from which the French Revolution sprang. The fanatic outcry of another philosopher, "We no more need a God", and the odious shibboleth "No God, no Master", of the Convention,—these were the sacrilegious watchwords which at that time heralded the liberation of man as an emancipation from all Divine Authority. And if, in His impenetrable wisdom, God employed that Revolution as a means by which to overthrow the tyranny of the Bourbons, and to bring a judgment on the princes who abused *His* nations as *their* footstool, nevertheless the principle of that Revolution remains thoroughly *anti-christian*, and has since spread like a cancer, dissolving and undermining all that stood firm and consistent before our Christian faith.

There is no doubt than that Christianity is imperilled by great and serious dangers. Two *life systems* 1) are

---

1) As DR. JAMES ORR (in his valuable lectures on *the Christian view of God and the world*, Edinb. 1897 p. 3) observes, the German technical term *Weltanschauung* has no precise equivalent in English. He therefore used the litteral translation *view of the world*, notwithstanding this phrase in English is limited by associations, which connect it predominatingly with *physical* nature. For this reason the more explicit phrase: *life and world view* seems to be preferable. My Americans friends however told me that the shorter phrase: *life system*, on the other side of the ocean, is often used in the same sense. So lecturing before an American public,

wrestling one with another, in mortal combat. Modernism is bound to build a world of its own from the data of the natural man, and to construct man himself from the data of nature; while, on the other hand, all those who reverently bend the knee to Christ and worship Him as the Son of the Living God, and God himself, are bent upon saving the "Christian Heritage". This is *the* struggle in Europe, this is *the* struggle in America, and this also, is the struggle for principles in which my own country is engaged, and in which I myself have been spending all my energy for nearly forty years.

In this struggle Apologetics have advanced us not one single step. Apologetics have invariably begun by abandoning the assailed breastwork, in order to entrench themselves cowardly in a ravelin behind it.

From the first therefore, I have always said to myself, —"If the battle is to be fought with honour and with a hope of victory, then *principle* must be arrayed against *principle;* then it must be felt that in Modernism the vast energy of an all-embracing *life-system* assails us, then also it must be understood that we have to take our stand in a life-system of equally comprehensive and far-reaching power. And this powerful life-system is not to be invented nor formulated by ourselves, but is to be taken and applied as it presents itself in history.

I took the shorter phrase, at least in the *title* of my first lecture, the shortest expression always having some preference for what is to be the general indication of your subject-matter. *In* my lectures on the contrary, I interchanged alternately both phrases, of *life-system* and *life and world view* in accordance with the special meaning predominating in my argumentation. See also DR. ORR's note on page 365.

When thus taken, I found and confessed, and I still hold, that this manifestation of the Christian principle is given us in *Calvinism*. In Calvinism my heart has found rest. From Calvinism have I drawn the inspiration, firmly and resolutely to take my stand in the thick of this great conflict of principles. And therefore, when I was invited most honourably by your Faculty to give the *Stone*-Lectures here this year, I could not hesitate a moment as to my choice of subject. Calvinism, as the only decisive, lawful, and consistent defence for Protestant nations against encroaching, and overwhelming Modernism,—this of itself was bound to be my theme.

Allow me therefore, in six lectures, to speak to you on Calvinism.

1. On Calvinism as a life system,
2. . On Calvinism and Religion,
3. On Calvinism and Politics,
4. On Calvinism and Science,
5. On Calvinism and Art,
and 6. On Calvinism and the Future.

Clearness of presentation demands that in this first lecture I begin by fixing the *conception* of Calvinism *historically*. To prevent misunderstanding we must first know what we should not, and what we should, understand by it. Starting therefore from the current use of the term, I find that this is by no means the same in different countries and in different spheres of life. The

name Calvinist is used in our times; first as a *sectarian*
name. This is not the case in Protestant, but in Roman
Catholic countries, especially in Hungary and France.
In Hungary the Reformed Churches have a membership
of some two and a-half millions, and in both the Romish
and Jewish press of that country her members are
constantly stigmatized by the non-official name of "Calvinists", a derisive name applied even to those who have
divested themselves of all traces of sympathy with the
faith of their fathers. The same phenomenon presents
itself in France, especially in the Southern parts, where
"Calviniste" is equally, and even more emphatically, a
sectarian stigma, which does not refer to the faith or
confession of the stigmatized person, but is simply put
upon every member of the Reformed Churches, even
though he be an atheist. George Thiébaud, known for
his anti-Semitic propaganda, has at the same time revived
the anti-Calvinistic spirit in France, and even in the
Dreyfus-case, "Jews and Calvinists" were arraigned by
him as the two anti-national forces, prejudicial to the
"esprit gaulois". — Directly opposed to this is the *second*
use of the word Calvinism, and this I call the *confessional* one. In this sense, a Calvinist is represented
exclusively as the outspoken subscriber to the dogma
of fore-ordination. They who disapprove of this strong
attachment to the doctrine of predestination coöperate
with the Romish polemists, in that by calling you
"Calvinist", they represent you as a victim of dogmatic
narrowness; and what is worse still, as being dangerous
to the real seriousness of moral life. This is a stigma
so conspicuously offensive that theologians like Hodge,

who from fulness of conviction were open defenders of Predestination, and counted it an honor to be Calvinists, were nevertheless so deeply impressed with the disfavour attached to the "Calvinistic name", that for the sake of commending their conviction, they prefered to speak rather of Augustinianism than of Calvinism. — The *denominational* title of some Baptists and Methodists indicates a *third* use of the name Calvinist. No less a man than Spurgeon belonged to a class of Baptists who in England call themselves "Calvinistic Baptists", and the Whitefield Methodists in Wales to this day bear the name of "Calvinistic Methodists". Thus here also it indicates in some way a confessional difference, but is applied as the name for special church-denominations. Without doubt this practice would have been most severely criticized by Calvin himself. During his life-time, no Reformed Church ever dreamed of naming the Church of Christ after any man. The Lutherans have done this, the Reformed Churches never. — But beyond this sectarian, confessional, and denominational use of the name "Calvinist", it serves moreover, in the *fourth* place, as a *scientific* name, either in an historical, philosophical or political sense. Historically, the name of Calvinism indicates the channel in which the Reformation moved, so far as it was neither Lutheran, nor Anabaptist nor Socinian. In the philosophical sense, we understand by it that system of conceptions which, under the influence of the master-mind of Calvin raised itself to dominance in the several spheres of life. And as a political name, Calvinism indicates that political movement which has guaranteed the liberty of nations

in constitutional statesmanship; first in Holland, then
in England, and since the close of the last century
in the United States. In this *scientific* sense, the name
of Calvinism is especially current among German scholars.
And the fact that this not only is the opinion of those
who are themselves of Calvinistic sympathies, but that
also scholars who have abandoned every confessional
standard of Christianity, nevertheless assign this profound
significance to Calvinism, appears from the testimony
borne by three of our best men of science, the first of
whom, Dr. Robert Fruin, declares that: "Calvinism
came into the Netherlands consisting of a logical system
of divinity, of a democratic Church-order of its own,
impelled by a severely-moral sense,. and as enthusiastic
for the moral as for the religious reformation of mankind". 1) Another historian, who was even more outspoken in his rationalistic sympathies, writes: "Calvinism
is the highest form of development reached by the
religious and political principle in the 16th century" 2).
And a third authority acknowledges that Calvinism has
liberated Switzerland, the Netherlands, and England, and

1) R. FRUIN, *Tien jaren uit den tachtigjarigen oorlog*, p. 151.

2) R. C. BAKHUIZEN VAN DEN BRINK, *Het huwelijk van Willem
van Oranje met Anna van Saxen*. 1853, p. 123: „Zoo al de laatste in
tijdorde, zoo was het Calvinisme de hoogste ontwikkelingsvorm van het
Godsdienstig-staatkundig beginsel der zestiende eeuw. Zelfs de regtzinnige
Staatkundigen dier eeuw, zagen met niet minder verachting en afschuw
neder op den Geneefschen regeeringsvorm — als men het in onze dagen
zou kunnen doen, wanneer een Staat het socialisme tot beginsel mogt
aannemen. Een hervormingskamp, die zoo laat na het ontstaan der
Hervorming kwam als dat bij ons, in Frankrijk en in Schotland plaats
had, kon niet anders dan Calvinistisch en ten voordeele van het Calvinisme zijn."

in the Pilgrim Fathers has provided the impulse to the prosperity of the United States. 1) Similarly Bancroft, among you, acknowledged that Calvinism "has a theory of ontology, of ethics, of social happiness, and of human liberty, all derived from God". 2) Only in this last-named, strictly scientific sense do I desire to speak to you on Calvinism as an independent general tendency, which from a mother-principle of its own, has developed an independent form both for our *life* and

1) Cd. Busken Huet, *Het Land van Rembrand*, 2e druk. II. p. 223. P. 159: „Was uit den aard der zaak de religie eene der hoofdzenuwen van den Kalvinistischen Staat" enz. (om andere redenen de negotie);

en p. 10, noot 3: „De geschiedenis van onze vrijwording is voor een groot gedeelte geschiedenis van onze hervorming, en de geschiedenis van onze hervorming is grootendeels geschiedenis van de uitbreiding van het Kalvinisme". Bakhuizen van den Brink, Studiën en Schetsen IV. 68. v. g.

2) *Hist. of the United States of America*, Ed. New York. II. p. 405. Cf. Von Polenz, *Geschichte des französischen Protestantismus*, 1857. I. p. VIII: Eine Geschichte ... in welcher der *Geist*, den Luther in Frankreich geweckt, dieses mit Eigenem und Fremden genährt und gefördert, Calvin aber gereinigt, geregelt, gehütet, gestärkt, fixirt und als ein bewegendes Ferment über die Schranken des Raums und der Verhältnisse weiter getrieben hat, der in seinen mannigfachen Strahlen alle geschichtlichen Momente mehr oder weniger berührenden *Brenn-* und *Lichtpunkt* bildet. Nennen wir diesen Geist, uneigentlich und anachronistisch zwar, aber, da er ohne Calvin sich verflüchtigt haben würde, nicht unwahr, *Calvinismus:* so ist meine Geschichte, ausser der des französischen Calvinismus im engeren und eigentlichen Sinne, die seiner einwirkung auf Religion, Kirche, Sitte, Gesellschaft und sonstige Verhältnissen Frankreichs.

C. G. Mc.Crie, *The public Worship of Presbyterian Scotland*, 1892. p. 95: It may lead some to attach value to these sentiments of Calvin if they know in what light the system which bears his stamp and his name is regarded by an Anglican Churchman of learning and insight, which give him a right to be heard in such a matter. "The

for our *thought* among the nations of Western Europe
and North America, and at present even in South
Africa.

The domain of Calvinism is indeed far broader than
the narrow confessional interpretation would lead us to
suppose. The aversion to naming the Church after a
man gave rise to the fact, that though in France the
Protestants were called "Huguenots", in the Netherlands .

Protestant movement", wrote Mark Pattison, "was saved from being sunk
in the quicksands of doctrinal dispute chiefly by the new moral direction
given to it in Geneva. "Calvinism saved Europe." "

P. HUME BROWN, *John Knox*, 1895. p. 252: Of all the developments
of Christianity, Calvinism and the Church of Rome alone bear the stamp
of an absolute religion.

P. 257. The difference between Calvin and Castalio, and between Knox
and the Ana-baptist, was not merely one of doctrine and dogma: their
essential difference lay in the spirit with which they respectively regarded
human society itself.

R. WILLIS, *Servetus and Calvin*, 1877. p. 514, 5: There can be little
question, in fact, that Calvinism, or some modification of its essential
principles, is the form of religious faith that has been professed in the
modern world by the most intelligent, moral, industrious, and freest of
mankind.

CHAMBERS, *Encyclopaedia*, Philadelphia, 1888. in voce Calvinism:
"With the revival of the evangelical party in the end of the century
Calvinism revived, and it still maintains, if not an absolute sway, yet a
powerful influence over many minds in the Anglican establishment. It is
one of the most living and powerful among the creeds of the Reformation.

DR. C. SYLVESTER HORNE, *Evang. Magazine*, Aug. 1898. *New Calvinism*,
p. 375 v. v. AND. DR. W. HASTIE, *Theology as Science*, Glasgow 1899.
p. 100—106: My apology and plea for the Reformed Theology, in presence
of the other theological tendencies of the time, have been founded upon
the two most general and fundamental points of creed that can be taken:
the universality of its basis in human nature, as the condition of its method,
and the universality of God, as the ground of its absolute truth.

"Beggars", in Great Britain "Puritans" and "Presbyterians", and in North America "Pilgrim Fathers", yet
all these products of the Reformation which on your
Continent and ours bore the special Reformed type, were
of Calvinistic origin. But the extent of the Calvinistic
domain should not be limited to these purer revelations.
Nobody applies such an exclusive rule to Christianity.
Within its boundaries we embrace not only Western
Europe, but also Russia, the Balkan States, the Armenians, and even Menelik's empire in Abyssinia. Therefore
it is but just that in the same way we should include in the
Calvinistic fold those churches also which have diverged
more or less from its purer forms. In her XXXIX
Articles, the Church of England is strictly Calvinistic,
even though in her Hierarchy and Liturgy she has
abandoned the straight paths, and has met with the
serious results of this departure in Puseyism and Ri-
tualism. The Confession of the Independents was equally
Calvinistic, even though in their conception of the Church
the organic structure was broken by individualism. And
if under the leadership of Wesley most Methodists became
opposed to the theological interpretation of Calvinism,
it is nevertheless the Calvinistic spirit itself that created
this spiritual reaction against the pertrifying church-life
of the times. In a given sense therefore it may be said,
that the entire field which in the end was covered by
the Reformation, so far as it was not Lutheran and
not Socinian, was dominated in principle by Calvinism.
Even the Baptists applied for shelter at the tents of
the Calvinists. It is the free character of Calvinism
that accounts for the rise of these several shades and

differences, and of the reactions against their excesses.
By its hierarchy, Romanism is and remains uniform.
Lutheranism owes its similar unity and uniformity to
the ascendency of the prince, whose relation to the
Church is that of "summus episcopus" and to its "ecclesia
docens". Calvinism on the other hand, which sanctions
no ecclesiastical hierarchy, and no magisterial interference,
could not develop itself except in many and varied forms .
and deviations, thereby of course incurring the danger
of degeneration, provoking in its turn all kind of one-
sided reactions. With the free development of life,
such as was intended by Calvinism, the distinction could
not fail to appear between a *centre*, with its fulness and
purity of vitality and strength, and the broad *circumference* with its threatening declensions. But in that
very conflict between a purer *centre* and a less pure
circumference the steady working of its spirit was
guaranteed to Calvinism.

Thus understood, Calvinism is rooted in a form of
religion which was peculiarly its own, and from this
specific religious consciousness there was developed first
a peculiar theology, then a special church-order, and
then a given form for political and social life, for the
interpretation of the moral world-order, for the relation
between nature and grace, between Christianity and
the world, between church and state, and finally for art
and science; and amid all these life-utterances it remained
always the self-same Calvinism, in so far as simultaneouly
and spontaneously all these developments sprang from
its deepest life-principle. Hence to this extent it stands
in line with those other great *complexes* of human life,

known as Paganism, Islamism and Romanism, by which we distinguish four entirely different worlds in the one collective world of human life. And if, speaking precisely, you should coordinate Christianity and not Calvinism with Paganism and Islamism, it is nevertheless better to place Calvinism in line with them, because Calvinism claims to embody the Christian idea more purely and accurately than could Romanism and Lutheranism. In the Greek world of Russia and the Balkan States, the national element is still dominant, and therefore the Christian faith in these countries has not yet been able to produce a form of life of its own from the root of its mystical orthodoxy. In Lutheran countries, the interference of the magistrate has prevented the free working of the spiritual principle. Hence of Romanism only can it be said, that it has embodied its life-thought in a world of conceptions and utterances entirely its own. But by the side of Romanism, and in opposition to it, Calvinism made its appearance, not merely to create a different Church-form, but an entirely different form for human life, to furnish human society with a different method of existence, and to populate the world of the human heart with different ideals and conceptions.

That this had not been realised until our time, and is now acknowledged by friend and enemy in consequence of a better study of history, should not surprise us. This would not have been the case, if Calvinism had entered life as a well-constructed system, and had presented itself as an outcome of study. But its origin came about in an entirely different way. In the order of existence, life is first. And to Calvinism life itself was ever the first object of its endeavours. There was too much to do and to suffer to devote much time to study. What was dominant was Calvinistic practice at the stake and in the field of battle. Moreover the nations among whom Calvinism gained the day,—such as the Swiss, the Dutch, the English and the Scotch—were by nature not very philosophically predisposed. Especially at that time, life among those nations was spontaneous and void of calculation; and only later on has Calvinism in its parts become a subject of that special study by which historians and theologians have traced the relation between Calvinistic phenomena and the all-embracing unity of its principle. It can even be said that the need of a theoretical and systematical study of so incisive and comprehensive a phenomenon of life, only arises when its first vitality has been exhausted, and when for the sake of maintaining itself in the future, it is compelled to greater accuracy in the drawing of its boundary lines. And if to this you add the fact that the stress of reflecting our existence as a unity in the mirror of our consciousness, is far stronger in our philosophical age than it ever was before, it is readily seen that both the needs of the present, and the care for the future, compel us to a deeper study of Calvinism. In the Roman Catholic Church everybody knows what he lives for, because with clear consciousness he enjoys the fruit of Rome's unity of life system. Even in Islâm you find the same power of a conviction of life dominated by one principle. Protestantism alone wanders about in the wilderness without aim or direction, moving hither and thither, without making any progress. This accounts for the fact that among Protestant nations Pantheism, born from the new German Philosophy and owing its concrete evolution-form to Darwin, claims for itself more and more the supremacy in every sphere of human life, even in that of theology, and under all sorts of names tries to overthrow our Christian traditions, and is bent even upon exchanging the heritage of our fathers for a hopeless modern Buddhism. The leading thoughts that had their rise in the French Revolution at the close of the last, and in German philosophy in the course of the present century, form together a life-system which is diametrically opposed to that of our fathers. Their struggles were for the sake of the glory of God and a purified Christianity; the present movement wages war for the sake of the glory of man being inspired, not by the humble mind of Golgotha but by the pride of Hero-worship. And why did we, Christians, stand so weak, in the face of this Modernism? Why did we constantly lose ground? Simply because we were devoid of an equal unity of life-conception, such as alone could· enable us with irresistible energy to repel the enemy at the frontier. This unity of life-conception, however, is never to be found in a vague conception of Protestantism winding itself as it does in all kind of tortuosities, but you do find it in that mighty historic process, which as Calvinism dug a channel of its own for the powerful stream of its life. By this unity of conception alone as given in Calvinism, you in America and we in Europe might be enabled once more to take our stand, by the side of Romanism, in opposition to

modern Pantheism. Without this unity of starting point
and life-system we must lose the power to maintain
our independent position, and our strength for resistance
must ebb away.

The supreme interest here at stake, however, forbids
our accepting without more positive proof the fact that
Calvinism really provides us with such an unity of life-
system and we demand proofs of the assertion that
Calvinism is not a partial nor was a merely temporary
phenomenon, but is such an all-embracing system of
principles, as, rooted in the past, is able to strengthen
us in the present and to fill us with confidence for the
future. Hence we must first ask what are the required
conditions for such general systems of life, as Paganism,
Islamism, Romanism and Modernism, and then show
that Calvinism really fulfils these conditions.

These conditions demand in the first place, that from
a special principle a peculiar insight be obtained into
the three fundamental relations of all human life; viz.,
1. our relation *to God*, 2. our relation *to man*, and 3.
our relation to *the world*.

Hence the first claim demands: that such a life system
shall find its starting-point in a special interpretation
of our relation to God. This is not accidental, but
imperative. If such an action is to put its stamp upon
our entire life, it must start from that point in our
consciousness, in which our life is still undivided and
lies comprehended in its unity,—not in the spreading
vines but in the root from which the vines spring.

This point, of course, lies in the antithesis between all that is finite in our human life and the infinite that lies beyond it. Here alone we find the common source from which the different streams of our human life spring and separate themselves. Personally it is our repeated experience that in the depths of our hearts, at the point where we disclose ourselves to the Eternal One, all the rays of our life converge as in one focus, and there alone regain that harmony, which we so often and so painfully lose in the stress of daily duty. In prayer lies not only our unity with God, but also the unity of our personal life. Movements in history, therefore, which do not spring from this deepest source are always partial and transient, and only those historical acts, which arose from these lowest depths of man's personal existence embrace the whole of life and possess the required permanence.

This was the case with *Paganism*, which in its most general form is known by the fact that it surmises, assumes and worships God *in the creature*. This applies to the lowest Animism, as well as to the highest Buddhism. Paganism does not rise to the conception of the independent existence of a God beyond and above the creature. But even in this imperfect form it has for its starting-point a definite interpretation of the relation of the infinite to the finite, and to this it owed its power to produce a finished form for human society. Simply because it possessed this significant starting-point was it able to produce a form of its own for the whole of human life.--It is the same with *Islamism*, which is characterized by its purely anti-pagan ideal, cutting

2

off all contact between the creature and God. Mohammed and the Korân are the historic names, but in its
nature the Crescent is the only absolute antithesis to
Paganism. Islâm *isolates God from the creature*, in order
to avoid all commingling with the creature. As *anti-
pode*, Islâm was possessed of an equally far-reaching
tendency, and was also able to originate an entirely
peculiar world of human life. — The same is the case
with *Romanism*. Here also the papal tiara, the hierarchy,
the mass, etc., are but the outcome of one fundamental
thought: viz., that God enters into fellowship with the
creature *by means of a mystic middle-link*, which is the
Church;—not taken as a mystic organism, but as a
visible, palpable and tangible institution. Here the Church
stands *between* God and the world, and so far as it
was able to adopt the world and to inspire it, Romanism
also created a form of its own for human society.—
And now, by the side of and opposite to these three,
Calvinism takes its stand with a fundamental thought
which is equally profound. It does not seek God *in*
the creature, as Paganism; it does not *isolate* God *from*
the creature, as Islamism; it posits no *mediate communion*
between God and the creature, as does Romanism; but
proclaims the exalted thought that, although standing
in high majesty above the creature, God enters *into
immediate fellowship with the creature*, as God the
Holy Spirit. This is even the heart and kernel of the
Calvinistic confession of predestination. There is communion with God, but only in entire accord with his
counsel of peace from all eternity. Thus there is no
grace but such as comes to us immediately from God.

At every moment of our existence, our entire spiritual
life rests in God Himself. The "Deo Soli Gloria" was
not the starting-point but the result, and predestination
was inexorably maintained, not for the sake of separating
man from man, nor in the interest of personal pride,
but in order to guarantee from eternity to eternity, to
our inner self, a direct and immediate communion with
the Living God. The opposition against Rome aimed
therefore with the Calvinist first of all at the dismissal
of a Church, which placed itself between the soul and
God. The Church consisted not in an office, nor in an
independent institute, the believers themselves were the
Church, inasmuch as by faith they stood in touch with
the Almighty. Thus, as in Paganism, Islamism and
Romanism, so also in Calvinism is found that proper,
definite interpretation of the fundamental relation of man
to God, which is required as the first condition of a
real life-system.

Meanwhile I anticipate two objections. In the first
place, it may be asked, whether I do not claim honours
for Calvinism which belong to Protestantism in general.
To this I reply in the negative. When I claim for
Calvinism the honour of having reestablished the direct
fellowship with God, I do not undervalue the general
significance of Protestantism. In the Protestant domain,
taken in the historic sense, Lutheranism alone stands
by the side of Calvinism. Now I wish to be second to
nome in my praises of Luther's heroic initiative. In his
heart, rather than in the heart of Calvin, was the bitter

conflict fought which led to the world-historic breach.
Luther can be interpreted without Calvin, but not
Calvin without Luther. To a great extent Calvin entered
upon the harvest of what the hero of Wittenberg had
sown in and outside Germany. But when the question
is put, Who had the clearest insight into the reformatory
principle, worked it out most fully, and applied it most
broadly, history points to the Thinker of Geneva and
not to the Hero of Wittenberg. Luther as well as Calvin
contended for a direct fellowship with God, but Luther
took it up from its subjective, anthropological side, and
not from its objective, cosmological side as Calvin did.
Luther's starting-point was the special-soteriological principle of a justifying faith; while Calvin's extending far
wider, lay in the general cosmological principle of the
sovereignty of God. As a natural result of this, Luther
also continued to consider the Church as the representative
and authoritative "teacher", standing between God and
the believer, while Calvin was the first to seek the
Church *in the believers themselves*. As far as he was
able, Luther still leaned upon the Romish view of the
sacraments, and upon the Romish cultus, while Calvin
was the first in both to draw the line which extended
immediately from God to man and from man to God.
Moreover, in all Lutheran countries the Reformation
originated from the princes rather than from the people,
and thereby passed under the power of the magistrate,
who took his stand in the Church officially as her
highest Bishop, and therefore was unable to change
either the social or the political life in accordance with
its principle. Lutheranism restricted itself to an exclu-

sively ecclesiastical and theological character, while Calvinism put its impress in and outside the Church upon every department of human life. Hence Lutheranism is nowhere spoken of as the creator of a peculiar lifeform; even the name of "Lutheranism" is hardly ever mentioned; while the students of history with increasing unanimity recognize Calvinism as the creator of a world of human life entirely its own.

The second objection, we have to meet is this: If it is true that every general development form of life must find its starting-point in a peculiar interpretation of our relation to God,—how then do you explain the fact, that *Modernism* also has led to such a general conception, notwithstanding it sprang from the French Revolution, which on principle broke with all religion. The question answers itself. If you exclude from your conceptions all reckoning with the Living God just as is implied in the cry, "no God no master", you certainly bring to the front a sharply defined interpretation of your own for our relation to God. A government, as you yourselves experienced of late in the case of Spain, that recalls its ambassador and breaks every regular intercourse with another power, declares thereby that its relation to the government of that country is a strained relation which generally ends in war. This is the case here. The leaders of the French Revolution, not being acquainted with any relation to God except that which existed trough the mediation of the Romish Church, annihilated all relation to God, because they wished to annihilate the power of the Church; and as a result of this they declared war against every religious

confession. But this of course very really implied a
fundamental and special interpretation of our relation
to God. It was the declaration that henceforth God
was to be considered as a *hostile power*, yea even as
dead, if not yet to the heart, at least to the state, to
society and to science. To be sure, in passing from
French into German hands, Modernism could not rest
content with such a bare negation; but the result shows
how from that moment it clothed itself in either pantheism or agnosticism, and under each disguise it maintained the expulsion of God from practical and theoretical
life, and the enmity against the Triune God had its full
course.

Thus I maintain that it is the interpretation of our
relation to God which dominates every general life
system, and that for us this conception is given in
Calvinism, thanks to its fundamental interpretation of an
immediate fellowship of God with man and of man with
God. To this I add that Calvinism has neither invented
nor conceived this fundamental interpretation, but that
God himself implanted it in the hearts of its heroes and
its heralds. We face here no product of a clever intellectualism, but the fruit of a work of God in the heart,
or, if you like, an inspiration of history. This point
should be emphasized. Calvinism has never burned its
incense upon the altar of genius, it has erected no
monument for its heroes, it scarcely calls them by
name. One stone only in a wall at Geneva remains to
remind one of Calvin. His very grave has been forgotten. Was this ingratitude? By no means. But if
Calvin was appreciated, even in the 16th and 17th

centuries the impression was vivid that it was One greater than Calvin, even God Himself, who had wrought here *His work*. Hence, no general movement in life is so devoid of deliberate compact, none so unconventional in which it spread as this. Simultaneously, Calvinism had its rise in all the countries of Western Europe, and it did not appear, among those nations, because the University was in its van, or because scholars led the people, or because a magistrate placed himself at their head; but it sprang from the hearts of the people themselves, with weavers and farmers, with tradesmen and servants, with women and young maidens; and in every instance it exhibited the same characteristic : viz., strong *Assurance of eternal Salvation*, not only without the intervention of the Church, but even in opposition to the Church. The human heart had attained unto eternal peace with its God: strengthened by this Divine fellowship, it discovered its high and holy calling to consecrate every department of life and every energy at its disposal to the glory of God: and therefore, when those men or women, who had become partakers of this Divine life, were forced to abandon their faith, it proved impossible, that they *could* deny their Lord; and thousands and tens of thousands burned at the stake, not complaining but exulting, with thanksgiving in their hearts and psalms upon their lips. Calvin was not the author of this, but God who through his Holy Spirit had wrought in Calvin that which He had wrought in them. Calvin stood not above them, but as a brother by their side, a sharer with them of God's blessing. In this way, Calvinism came to its fundamental interpretation of an

immediate fellowship with God, not because Calvin
invented it, but because in this immediate fellowship
God Himself had granted to our fathers a privilege of
which Calvin was only the first to become clearly
conscious. This is the great work of the Holy Spirit
in history, by which Calvinism has been consecrated,
and which interprets to us its wondrous energy.

There are times in history when the pulse of religious
life beats faintly; but there are times when its beat is
bounding, and the latter was the case in the 16th century
among the nations of Western Europe. The question
of faith at that time dominated every activity in public
life. New history starts out from this *faith*, even as
the history of our times starts from the *unbelief* of the
French Revolution. What law this pulse-like movement
of religious life obeys, we cannot tell, but it is evident
that there is such a law, and that in times of high
religious tension the inworking of the Holy Spirit upon
the heart is irresistible; and this mighty inworking of
God was the experience of our Calvinists, Puritans and
Pilgrim Fathers. It was not in all individuals to the
same degree, for this never happens in any great movement; but they who formed the centre of life in those
times, who were the promotors of that mighty change,
they experienced this higher power to the fullest: and
they were the men and women of every class of society
and nationality who by God Himself were admitted
into communion with the majesty of His eternal Being.
Thanks to this work of God in the heart, the persuasion
that the whole of a man's life is to be lived as *in the
Divine Presence* has become the fundamental thought

of Calvinism. By this decisive idea, or rather by this mighty fact, it has allowed itself to be controlled in every department of its entire domain. It is from this mother-thought that the all-embracing life system of Calvinism sprang.

This brings us of itself to the second condition, with which, for the sake of creating a life system every profound movement has to comply: viz., a fundamental interpretation of its own touching *the relation of man to man*. How we stand toward God is the first, and how we stand toward man is the second principal question, which decides the tendency and the construction of our life. There is no uniformity among men, but endless multiformity. In creation itself the difference has been established between woman and man. Physical and spiritual gifts and talents cause one person to differ from the other. Past generations and our own personal life create distinctions. The social position of the rich and poor differs widely. Now, these differences are in a special way *weakened* or *accentuated* by every consistent life system, and Paganism and Islamism, Romanism as well as Modernism, and so also Calvinism have all taken their stand in this question in accordance with their primordial principle. If, as Paganism contends, God dwells *in* the creature, a divine superiority is exhibited in whatever is high among men. In this way it obtained its demigods, hero-worship, and finally its sacrifices upon the altar of Divus Augustus. On the other hand whatever is lower is considered as godless,

and therefore gives rise to the systems of caste in India
and in Egypt, and to slavery everywhere else, thereby
placing one man under a base subjection to his fellow-
man.   Under Islamism, which dreams of its paradise of
houries, sensuality usurps public authority, and woman
is the slave of man, even as the kafir is the slave of
the Moslim. Romanism, taking root in Christian soil,
overcomes the absolute character of distinction, and renders it relative, in order to interpret every relation of
man to man *hierarchically*. There is a hierarchy among
the angels of God, a hierarchy in God's Church, and
so also a hierarchy among men, leading to an entirely
aristocratic interpretation of life as the embodiment of
the ideal. Finally Modernism, which denies and abol-
ishes every difference, cannot rest until it has made
woman man and man woman, and, putting every distinction on a common level, kills life by placing it under
the ban of uniformity. One type must answer for all,
one uniform, one position and one and the same development of life; and whatever goes beyond and above
it, is looked upon as an insult to the common consciousness. In the same way Calvinism has derived from
its fundamental relation to God a peculiar interpretation
of man's relation to man, and it is this only true
relation, which since the 16th century has ennobled social
life. If Calvinism places our entire human life immediately before God, then it follows that all men or
women, rich or poor, weak or strong, dull or talented,
as creatures of God, and as lost sinners, have no claim
whatsoever to lord over one another, and that we stand
as equals before God, and consequently equal as man

to man. Hence we cannot recognize any distinction among men, save such as has been imposed by God Himself, in that He gave one authority over the other, or enriched one with more talents than the other, in order that the man of more talents should serve the man with less, and in him serve his God. Hence Calvinism condemns not merely all open slavery and systems of caste, but also all covert slavery of woman and of the poor; it is opposed to all hierarchy among men; it tolerates no aristocracy save such as is able, either in person or in family, by the grace of God, to exhibit superiority of character or talent, and to show that it does not claim this superiority for self-aggrandizement or ambitious pride, but for the sake of spending it in the service of God. So Calvinism was bound to find its utterance in the democratic interpretation of life; to proclaim the liberty of nations; and not to rest until both politically and socially every man, simply because he is man, should be recognized, respected and dealt with as a creature created after the Divine likeness.

This was no outcome of envy. It was not the man of lower estate who reduced his superior to his level in order to usurp the higher place, but it was all men kneeling in concert at the feet of the Holy One of Israel. This accounts for the fact that Calvinism made no sudden break with the past. Even as in its early stage Christianity did not abolish slavery, but undermined it by a moral judgment, so Calvinism allowed the provisional continuance of the conditions of hierarchy and aristocracy as traditions belonging to the Middle Ages. It was not charged against William of Orange, that

he was a prince of royal lineage; he was the more
honoured for it. But inwardly Calvinism has modified the
structure of society, not by the envying of classes, nor
by an undue esteem for the possessions of the rich,
but by a more serious interpretation of life. By better
labor and a higher development of character the middle
and working classes have provoked the nobility and the
wealthier citizens to jealousy. First looking to God,
and then to one's neighbour was the impulse, the mind
and the spiritual custom to which Calvinism gave entrance.
And from this holy fear of God and this united stand
before the face of God a holier democratic idea has
developed itself, and has continually gained ground.
This result has been brought about by nothing so much
as by fellowship in suffering. When, though loyal to
the Romish faith, the dukes of Egmont and Hoorn
ascended the same scaffold on which, for the sake of
a nobler faith, the working-man and the weaver had
been executed, the reconciliation between the classes
received its sanction in that bitter death. By his bloody
persecutions, Alva the Aristocrat advanced the pros-
perous development of the spirit of Democracy. To
have placed man on a footing of equality with man,
so far as the purely human interests are concerned, is
the immortal glory which incontestably belongs to Calvinism. The difference between it and the wild dream
of equality of the French Revolution is : that while in
Paris it was one action in concert *against* God, here
all, rich and poor, were on their knees *before* God,
consumed with a common zeal for the glory of His Name,

The third fundamental relation which decides the interpretation of life is the relation which you bear *to the
world*. As previously stated there are three principal
elements with which you come into touch: viz., God,
man and the world. The relation to God and to man
into which Calvinism places you being thus reviewed,
the third and last fundamental relation is in order: viz.,
your attitude *toward the world*. Of Paganism it can be
said in general, that it places *too high* an estimate upon
the world, and therefore to some extent it both stands
in fear of, and loses itself in it. On the other hand
Islamism places *too low* an estimate upon the world,
makes sport of it and triumphs over it in reaching after
the visionary world of a sensual paradise. For the
purpose in view however we need say no more of
either, since both for Christian Europe and America
the antithesis between man and the world has assumed
the narrower form of the antithesis between the world
and the Christian circles. The traditions of the Middle
Ages gave rise to this. Under the hierarchy of Rome
the Church and the World were placed over against
each other, the one as being sanctified and the other
as being still under the curse. Everything outside the
Church was under the influence of demons, and exorcism
banished this demoniacal power from everything that
came under the protection, influence and inspiration of
the Church. Hence in a Christian country the entire
social life was to be covered by the wings of the Church.
The magistrate had to be anointed and confessionally
bound; art and science had to be placed under ecclesiastical encouragement and censure, trade and commerce

had to be bound to the Church by the tie of guilds; and
from the cradle to the grave family-life was to be placed
under ecclesiastical guardianship. This was a gigantic
effort to claim the entire world for Christ, but one which
of necessity brought with it the severest judgment upon
every life-tendency which either as heretical or as
demoniacal withdrew itself from the blessing of the
Church. Hence the stake was fit alike for witch and
heretic, for in principle both lay under the same ban.
And this deadening theory was carried out with iron
logic, not from cruelty, nor from any low ambition, but
from the lofty purpose of saving the christianized world,
i.e., the world as overshadowed by the Church. Escape
from the world was the counterpoise in monastic and
partly even in clerical orders, which emphasized holiness
in the centrum of the Church in order to wink the
more lightly at worldly excesses without. As a natural
result the world corrupted the Church, and by its
dominion over the world the Church proved an obstacle
to every free development of its life.

Thus making its appearance in a dualistic social state
Calvinism has wrought an entire change in the world
of thoughts and conceptions. In this also, placing itself
before the face of God, it has not only honored *man*
for the sake of his likeness to the Divine image, but
also *the world* as a Divine creation, and has at once
placed to the front the great pinciple that there is a
particular grace which works Salvation, and also a
common grace by which God, maintaining the life of
the world, relaxes the curse which rests upon it, arrests
its process of corruption, and thus allows the untram-

melled development of our life in which to glorify Himself as Creator. Thus the Church receded in order to be neither more nor less than the congregation of believers, and in every department the life of the world was not emancipated from God, but from the dominion of the Church. Thus domestic life regained its independence, trade and commerce realized their strength in liberty, art and science were set free from every ecclesiastical bond and restored to their own inspirations, and man began to understand the subjection of all nature with its hidden forces and treasures to himself as a holy duty, imposed upon him by the original ordinances of Paradise: "Have dominion over them". Henceforth the curse should no longer rest upon the *world* itself, but upon that which is *sinful* in it, and instead of monastic flight *from* the world the duty is now emphasized of serving God *in* the world, in every position in life. To praise God in the Church and serve Him in the world became the inspiring impulse, and, in the Church, strength was to be gathered by which to resist temptation and sin in the world. Thus puritanic sobriety went hand in hand with the reconquest of the entire life of the world, and Calvinism gave the impulse to that new development which dared to face the world with the Roman thought: *nil humanum a me alienum puto*, although never allowing itself to be intoxicated by its poisonous cup.

Especially in its antithesis to Anabaptism Calvinism exhibits itself in bold relief. For Anabaptism adopted the opposite method, and in its effort to evade the world it confirmed the monastic starting-point, general-

ising and making it a rule for *all* believers. It was not
from Calvinism, but from this anabaptistic principle, that
Akosmism had its rise among so many Protestants in
Western Europe. In fact Anabaptism adopted the Romish theory, with this difference: that it placed the
kingdom of God in the room of the Church, and abandoned the distinction between the two moral standards,
one for the clergy and the other for the laity. For
the rest the Anabaptist's standpoint was: 1. that the
unbaptized world was under the curse, for which reason
he withdrew from all civil institutions; and 2. that the
circle of baptized believers—with Rome the Church, but
with him the kingdom of God—was in duty bound to
take all civil life under its guardianship and to remodel
it; and so John of Leyden violently established his
shameless power at Munster as King of the *New Zion*,
and his devotees ran naked through the streets of Amsterdam. Hence, on the same grounds on which Calvinism rejected Rome's theory concerning the world, it
rejected the theory of the Anabaptist, and proclaimed
that the Church must withdraw again within its spiritual
domain, and that in the world we should realize the
potencies of God's common grace.

Thus it is shown that Calvinism has a sharply-defined
starting-point of its own for the three fundamental relations of all human existence: viz., our relation to *God*,
to *man* and to the *world*. For our relation *to God*:
an immediate fellowship of man with the Eternal, independently of priest or church. For the relation of man
to man: the recognition in each person of human worth,
which is his by virtue of his creation after the Divine

likeness, and therefore of the equality of all men before
God and his magistrate. And for our relation *to the
world:* the recognition that in the whole world the curse
is restrained by grace, that the life of the world is to
be honored in its independence, and that we must, in
every domain, discover the treasures and develop the
potencies hidden by God in nature and in human life.
This justifies us fully in our statement that Calvinism
duly answers the three above named conditions, and
thus is incontestably entitled to take its stand by the
side of Paganism, Islamism, Romanism and Modernism,
and to claim for itself the glory of possessing a well-
defined principle and an all-embracing life-system.

But even this is not all. The fact that in a given
circle Calvinism has formed an interpretation of life
quite its own, from which both in the spiritual and
secular domain a special system arose for domestic and
social life, justifies its claim to assert itself as an independent formation ; but does not yet credit it with the
honour of having led humanity, as such, up to a higher
stage in its development, and therefore this life-system
has not, so far as we have yet considered it, attained
that position which alone could give it the right to
claim for itself the energy and devotion of our hearts.
In China it can be asserted with equal right that
Confucianism has produced a form of its own for life
in a given circle, and with the Mongolian race that
form of life rests upon a théory of its own. But what
has China done for humanity in general, and for the

steady development of our race? Even so far as the
waters of its life were clear, they formed nothing but
an isolated lake. Almost the same remark applies to
the high development which was once the boast of India
and to the state of things in Mexico and Peru in the
days of Montezuma and the Incas. In all these regions
the people attained a high degree of development, but
stopped there, and, remaining isolated, in no way proved
a benefit to humanity at large. This applies more
strongly still to the life of the coloured races on the
coast and in the interior of Africa — a far lower form
of existence, reminding us not even of a lake but rather
of pools and marshes. There is but one world-stream,
broad and fresh, which from the beginning bore the
promise of the future. This stream had its rise in Middle-
Asia and the Levant, and has steadily continued its
course from East to West. From Western Europe it
has passed on to your Eastern States and from thence
to California. The sources of this stream of development are found in Babylon and in the valley of the
Nile. From thence it flowed on to Greece. From
Greece it passed on to the Roman Empire. From
the Romanic nations it continued its way to the North-
western parts of Europe, and from Holland and England
it reached at length your continent. At present that
stream is at a standstill. Its Western course through
China and Japan is impeded; meanwhile no one can
tell what forces for the future may yet lie slumbering
in the Slavic races which have thus far failed of progress. But while this secret of the future is still veiled
in mystery, the course of this world-stream from East

to West can be denied by none. And therefore I am justified in saying: that Paganism, Islamism and Romanism are the three successive formations which this development had reached, when its further direction passed over into the hands of Calvinism; and that Calvinism in turn is now denied this leading influence by Modernism, the daughter of the French Revolution.

The succession of these four phases of development did not take place mechanically, with sharply outlined divisions and parts. This development of life is organic, and therefore each new period roots in the past. In its deepest logic Calvinism had already been apprehended by Augustine; had, long before Augustine, been proclaimed to the City of the seven hills by the Apostle in his Epistle to the Romans; and from Paul goes back to Israel and its prophets, yea to the tents of the patriarchs. Romanism likewise does not make its appearance suddenly, but is the joint product of the three potencies of Israel's priesthood, the cross of Calvary, and the world-organization of the Roman Empire. Islâm in the same way joins itself to Israel's Monism, to the Prophet of Nazareth, and to the tradition of the Koraishites. And even the Paganism of Babylon and Egypt on the one hand, and of Greece and Rome upon the other, stand organically related to what lay behind these nations, preceding the prosperity of their lives. But even so, it is as clear as day that the supreme force in the central development of the human race moved along successively from Babylon and Egypt to Greece and Rome, then to the chief regions of the Papal dominion, and finally to the Calvinistic nations

of Western Europe. If Israel flourished in the days
of Babylon and Egypt, however high its standard, the
direction and the development of our human race was
not in the hands of the sons of Abraham but in
those of the Belshassars and the Pharaohs. Again, this
leadership does not pass from Babylon and Egypt on
to Israel but to Greece and Rome. However high the
stream of Christianity had risen when Islàm made its
appearance, in the 8th and 9th centuries the followers
of Mahomet were our teachers and with *them* rested
the issue of the world. And though the hegemony of
Romanism still maintained itself for a short time after
the peace of Munster, no one questions the fact, that
the higher development, which we are now enjoying, we
owe neither to Spain nor to Austria, nor even to the
Germany of that time, but to the Calvinistic countries
of the Netherlands and to England of the 16th century.
Under Louis XIV, Romanism arrested this higher development in France, but only that in the French Revolution
it might exhibit a ghastly caricature of Calvinism, which in
its sad consequences broke the inner strength of France
as a nation, and weakened its international significance.
The fundamental idea of Calvin has been transplanted
from Holland and England to America, thus driving
our higher development ever more Westward, until on
the shores of the Pacific it now reverently awaits whatsoever God has ordained. But no matter what mysteries
the future may yet have to disclose, the fact remains
that the broad stream of the development of our race
runs from Babylon to San Francisco, through the five
stadia of Babylonian-Egyptian, Greek-Roman, Islamitic,

Romanistic and Calvinistic civilization, and the present conflict in Europe as well as in America finds its main cause in the fundamental antithesis between the energy of Calvinism which proceded from the throne of God, found the source of its power in the Word of God, and in every sphere of human life exalted the glory of God,—and its carricature in the French Revolution, which proclaimed its unbelief in the cry of, "no God no master"; and which presently in the form of German Pantheism is reducing itself more and more to a modern Paganism.

————

Thus notice I was not too bold, when I claimed for Calvinism the honour of being neither an ecclesiastical, nor a theological, nor a sectarian conception, but one of the principal phases in the general development of our human race; and among these the youngest, whose high calling still is to influence the further course of human life.—Just now, however, allow me to indicate another circumstance, which strengthens my principal statement, viz., *the commingling of blood* as, thus far, the physical basis of all higher human development. From the high-lands of Asia our human race came down in groups, and these in turn have been divided into races and nations; and in entire conformity to the prophetic blessing of Noah the children of Shem and of Japheth have been the sole bearers of the development of the race. No impulse for any higher life has ever gone forth from the third group. With the two other groups a twofold phenomenon presents itself. There are tribal nations which have *isolated* themselves and others which have *intermingled*. Thus on the one hand there are groups which have dominated exclusively their own inherent forces, and on the other hand groups which by commingling have crossed their traits with those of other tribes, and thus have attained a higher perfection. It is noteworthy that the process of human development steadily proceeds with those groups whose historic characteristic is not isolation but the commingling . of blood. On the whole the Mongolian race has held itself apart, and in its isolation has bestowed no benefits upon our race at large. Behind the Himalayas a similar life secluded itself, and hence failed to impart any permanent impulse to the outside world. Even in Europe we find that with the Scandinavians and Slavs there was hardly any intermingling of blood, and, consequently having failed to develop a richer type, they have taken little part in the general development of human life. On the other hand the tablets from Babylon in our great Museums by the two languages of their inscriptions still show that in Mesopotamia the Aryan element of the Accadians mingled itself at an early period with the Semitic-Babylonian ; and Egyptology leads us to conclude that in the land of the Pharaohs we deal from the beginning with a population produced by the mingling of two very different tribes. No one believes any longer the pretended race-unity of the Greeks. In Greece as well as in Italy we deal with races of a later date who have intermingled with the earlier Pelasgians, Etruscians and others. Islàm seems to be exclusively Arabic, but a study of the spread of Islamism among the Moors, Persians, Turks and other series of subjected tribes, with whom intermarriage was common, at once reveals the fact that especially with Mahometans the commingling of blood was even greater than with their predecessors. When the leadership of the world passed into the hands of the Romanic nations, the same phenomenon presented itself in Italy, Spain, Portugal and France. In these cases the Aborigines were generally Basques or Celts, the Celts in turn being overcome by the Germanic tribes, and even as in Italy the East Goths and Lombards, so in Spain the West-Goths, in Portugal the Swabians and in France the Franks instilled new blood into debilitated veins, and to this wonderful rejuvenescence the Romanic nations owed their vigour until far into the 16th century. Thus in the life of nations the same phenomenon repeats itself which so often strikes the Historian as a result of international marriages among princely families, as we see how the Habsburgs and the Bourbons, the Oranges and the Hohenzollern, for instance, have been, century after century, productive of a host of most remarkable statesmen and heroes. The raiser of stock has aimed at the same effect in the crossing of different breeds, and botanists harvest large profits by obeying the same law of life with plants; and by itself it is not difficult to perceive that the union of natural powers, divided among different tribes, must be productive of a higher development. To this it should be added that the history of our race does not aim at the improvement of any single tribe, but at the development of *mankind* taken as a whole, and therefore needs this commingling of blood in order to attain its end. Now in fact history shows that the nations among whom Calvinism flourished most

widely, exhibit in every way this same mingling of
races. In Switzerland, the Germans, united with Italians
and French; in France, the Gauls, with Franks and
Burgundians; in the Lowlands, Celts and Welch with
Germans; also in England the old Celts and Anglo-
saxons were afterwards raised to a still higher standard
of national life by the invasion of the Normans. Indeed
it may be said, that the three principal tribes of Western
Europe, the Celtic, Romanic and Germanic elements
under the leadership of the Germanic, give us the
genealogy of the Calvinistic nations. In America, where
Calvinism has come to unfold itself in a still higher
liberty, this commingling of blood is assuming a larger
proportion than has ever yet been known. Here the
blood flows together from all the tribes of the ancient
world, and again we have the Celts from Ireland, the
Germans from Germany and Scandinavia, united to the
Slavs from Russia and Poland, who promote still
further this already vigorous intermingling of the races.
This latter process takes place under the higher ex-
ponent that it is not merely the union of tribe with
tribe, but that the old historic nations are dissolving
themselves in order to allow the re-union of their
members in one higher unity, hitherto constantly assi-
milated by the American type. In this respect also
Calvinism fully meets the conditions imposed on every
new phase of development in the life of humanity. It
spread itself in a domain where it found the commingling
of blood stronger than under Romanism, and in America
raised this to its highest conceivable realization.

Thus it is shown that Calvinism meets not only the necessary condition of the mingling of blood, but that in the process of human development it also represents, with respect to this, a further stadium. In Babylon this commingling of blood was of small significance; it gains in importance with the Greeks and Romans; it goes further under Islamism; is dominant under Romanism; but only among Calvinistic nations does it reach its highest perfection. Here in America it is achieving the intermingling of *all* the nations of the old world. A similar climax of this process of human development is also exhibited by Calvinism in the fact, that only under the influence of Calvinism does the impulse of public activity proceed from the people themselves. In the life of the nations also there is development from the underage period to that of maturity. As in the family-life, during the years of childhood, the direction of affairs is in the hands of the parents, so also in the life of the nations it is but natural that during their under-age period first the Asiatic despot, then some eminent ruler, afterwards the priesthood, and finally both priest and magistrate together should stand at the head of every movement. The history of the nations in Babylon and under the Pharaohs, in Greece and Rome, under Islamism and under the papal system, fully confirms this course of development. But it is self-evident that this could not be a permanent state of things. Just because in their progressive development the nations finally came of age, they must at length reach that stadium in which the people itself awoke, stood up for their rights, and originated the movement

that was to direct the course of future events; and in
the rise of Calvinism *this* stadium appears to have been
reached. Thus far every forward movement had gone
forth from the authorities in State, Church or Science,
and from thence had descended to the people. In Calvinism on the other hand the peoples themselves stand
out in their broad ranks and from a spontaneity of
their own, press forward to a higher form of social
life and conditions. Calvinism had its rise *with the
people*. In Lutheran countries the magistrate was still
the leader in public advances, but in Switzerland, among
the Huguenots, in Belgium, in the Netherlands, in
Scotland and also in America the peoples themselves
created the impetus. They seemed to have matured;
to have reached the period in which they were of age.
Even when in some cases, as in the Netherlands, the
nobility for a moment took an heroic stand for the
oppressed, their activity ended in nothing, and the
people alone, by undaunted energy, broke the barrier,
and among these it was the "common folk" to whose
heroic initiative William the Silent, as he himself acknowledges, owed the success of his undertaking.

Hence as a central phenomenon in the development
of humanity Calvinism is not only entitled to an
honourable position by the side of Paganistic, Islamistic
and Romanistic forms, since like these it represents a
peculiar principle dominating the whole of life, but it
also meets every required condition for the advancement
of human development *to a higher stage*. And yet

this would remain a bare possibility without any corresponding reality, if history did not testify that Calvinism has *actually* caused the stream of human life to flow in another channel, and has ennobled the social life of the nations. And therefore in closing I assert that Calvinism not only held out these possibilities but has also understood how to realize them. To prove this, just ask yourselves what would have become of Europe and America, if in the 16th century the star of Calvinism had not suddenly arisen on the horizon of Western Europe. In that case Spain would have crushed the Netherlands. In England and Scotland the Stuarts would have carried out their fatal plans. In Switzerland the spirit of half-heartedness would have gained the day. The beginnings of life in this new world would have been of an entirely different character. And as an unavoidable sequence the balance of power in Europe would have returned to its former position. Protestantism would not have been able to maintain itself in politics. No further resistance could have been offered to the Romish-conservative power of the Habsburgs, the Bourbons and the Stuarts; and the free development of the nations, as seen in Europe and America, would simply have been prevented. The whole American continent would have remained subject to Spain. The history of both continents would have become a most mournful one and it ever remains a question whether the spirit of the Leipzig Interim would not have succeded, by way of a Romanized Protestantism, in reducing Northern Europe again to the sway of the old Hierarchy. The enthusiastic devotion of the best historians of the second

half of this century to the struggle of the Netherlands
against Spain, as one of the finest subjects of investigation, only explains itself by the conviction, that if
the power of Spain at that time had not been broken
by the heroism of the Calvinistic spirit, the history of
the Netherlands, of Europe and of the world would have
been as painfully sad and dark as now, thanks to
Calvinism, it is bright and inspiriting. Professor Fruin
justly remarks that: "In Switzerland, in France, in the
Netherlands, in Scotland and in England, and wherever
Protestantism has had to establish itself at the point of
the sword, it was Calvinism that gained the day."

Call to mind that this turn in the history of the
world could not have been brought about except by the
implanting of another principle in the human heart, and
by the disclosing of another world of thought to the
human mind; that only by Calvinism the psalm of
liberty found its way from the troubled conscience to
the lips; that Calvinism has captured and guaranteed
to us our constitutional civil rights; and that simultaneously with this there went out from Western Europe
that mighty movement which promoted the revival of
science and art, opened new avenues to commerce and
trade, beautified domestic and social life, exalted the
middle classes to positions of honor, caused philanthropy
to abound, and more than all this, elevated, purified
and ennobled moral life by puritanic seriousness;
and then judge for yourselves whether it will do to
banish any longer this God-given Calvinism to the
archives of history, and whether it is so much of a
dream to conceive that Calvinism has yet a blessing

to bring and a bright hope to unveil for the future.

The struggle of the Boers in the Transvaal against one of the mightiest powers must often have reminded you of your own past. In what has been achieved at Majuba, and recently at the occasion of Jameson's raid the heroism of old Calvinism was again brilliantly evident. If Calvinism had not been passed on from our fathers to their African descendants, no free republic would have arisen in the South of the Dark Continent. This proves that Calvinism is not dead—that it still carries in its germ the vital energy of the days of its former glory. Yea, even as a grain of wheat from the Sarcophagi of the Pharaohs, when again committed to the soil, bears fruit a hundredfold, so Calvinism still carries in itself a wondrous power for the future of the nations. And if we, Christians of both Continents, in our still holier struggle, are still expected to achieve heroic deeds, marching under the banner of the Cross against the spirit of the times, Calvinism alone arms us with an inflexible principle, by the strength of that principle guaranteeing us a sure, though far from easy victory.

CALVINISM AND RELIGION.*

The conclusion arrived at in my previous Lecture, was first, that, scientifically speaking, Calvinism means the completed evolution of Protestantism, resulting in a both higher and richer stage of human development. Further, that the world-view of Modernism, with its starting-point in the French Revolution, can claim no higher privilege than that of presenting an atheistic imitation of the brilliant ideal proclaimed by Calvinism, therefore being unqualified for the honour of leading us higher on. And, lastly, that whosoever rejects atheism as his fundamental thought, is bound to go back to Calvinism, not to restore its worn-out form, but once more to catch hold of the Calvinistic principles, in order to embody them in such a form as, suiting the requirements of our own century, may restore the needed unity to Protestant thought and the lacking energy to Protestant practical life.

In my present Lecture, therefore, treating of *Calvinism and Religion*, first of all I will try to illustrate the dominant position occupied by Calvinism in the central domain of our worship of the Most High. The fact that, in the religious domain, Calvinism *has* occupied from the first a peculiar and impressive position, nobody will deny. As if by one magical stroke, it created its own Confession, its own Theology, its own Church Organisation, its own Church Discipline, its own Cultus, and its own Moral Praxis. And continued historical investigation proves with increasing certainty that all these new Calvinistic forms for our religious life were the logical product of its own fundamental thought and the embodiment of one and the same principle. Measure the energy which Calvinism here displayed by the utter incapability Modernism evinced in the same domain by the absolute fruitlessness of its endeavours. Ever since it entered its "mystical" period, Modernism also, both in Europe and in America, has acknowledged the necessity of carving out a new form for the religious life of our time. Hardly a century after the once glittering tinsel of Rationalism, now that Materialism is sounding its retreat in the ranks of science, a kind of hollow piety is again exercising its enticing charms, and every day it is becoming more fashionable to take a plunge into the warm stream of mysticism. With an almost sensual delight this modern mysticism quaffs its intoxicating draught from the nectar-cup of some intangible infinite. It was even purposed that, on the ruins of the once so stately Puritanic building, a new religion, with a new ritual should be inaugurated, as a higher evolution of religious life. Already, for more than a quarter of a century, the dedication and solemn opening of this

new sanctuary has been promised us. And yet it has
all led to nothing. No tangible effect has been produced.
No formative principle has emerged from the imbroglio
of hypotheses. Not even the beginning of an associative
movement is as yet perceptible, and the long looked
for plant has not even lifted its head above the barren
soil.—Now, in contraposition to this, look at the giant
spirit of Calvin, who, in the sixteenth century, with one
master-stroke, placed before the gaze of the astonished
world an entire religious edifice, erected in the purest
Scriptural style. So rapidly was the whole building
completed that most of the spectators forgot to pay
attention to the wonderful structure of the foundations.
In all that the religious modern thought has, I will
not say created, as with a master hand, but heaped
together, like an unsuccessful amateur,—not one nation,
not one family, hardly one solitary soul has (to use
Augustine's words), ever found the *requiescat* for his
"broken heart," while the Reformer of Geneva, by his
mighty spiritual energy, unto five nations at once, both
then, and after the lapse of three centuries, has afforded
guidance in life, the uplifting of the heart unto the Father
of Spirits, and holy peace, for ever. This naturally leads
to the question—what was the secret of this wonderful
energy? Allow me to present the answer to this question,—first in *Religion as such*, next in religion as manifested in the *Life of the Church*, and lastly in the
fruit of Religion for *Practical Life*.

———

First, then, we must consider *Religion as such*.

Here four mutually dependent fundamental questions arise ;—1. Does Religion exist for the sake of *God*, or for *Man?* 2. Must it operate *directly* or *mediately?* 3. Can it remain *partial* in its operations or has it to embrace the *whole* of our personal being and existence? and, 4. Can it bear a *normal*, or must it reveal an *abnormal*, *i. e.*, a soteriological character? To these four questions Calvinism answers : 1. Man's religion ought to be not egotistical, and for *man*, but ideal, for the sake of *God*. 2. It has to operate not *mediately*, by human interposition, but *directly*, from the heart. 3. It may not remain *partial*, as running alongside of life, but must lay hold upon our *whole* existence. And 4. Its character should be soteriological, *i. e.*, it should spring, not from our *fallen* nature, but from the *new man*, restored by palingenesis to his original standard.

Allow me then successively to elucidate each of these four points.

Modern religious philosophy ascribes the origin of religion to a potency, from which it could not originate, but which acted merely, as its supporter and preserver. It has mistaken the dead prop of the living shoot for the living shoot itself. Attention is called, and very properly, to the contrast between man, and the overwhelming power of the cosmos which surrounds him; and now religion is introduced as a mystical energy, trying to strengthen him against this immense power of the cosmos which inspires him with such deadly fear. Being conscious of the dominion which his unseen soul exercises over his own tangible body, he infers quite naturally, that Nature, also, must be moved by the impulse of some hidden spiritual power. Animistically, therefore, he first explains the movements of nature as the result of an indwelling army of spirits, and tries to catch them, to conjure them, to bend them to his advantage. Then, rising from this atomistic idea to a more comprehensive conception, he begins to believe in the existence of personal gods, expecting from these divine beings, who stand above nature, effectual assistance against the fiendish power of Nature. And finally, grasping the contrast between the spiritual and the material, he pays homage to the Supreme Spirit, as standing over against all that is visible, till, in the end, having abandoned his faith in such an extramundane Spirit, as a personal being, and charmed by the loftiness of his own human spirit, he prostrates himself before some impersonal ideal, of which in self adoration he deems himself to be the worshipful incarnation. But whatever may be the various stages in the progress of this egoistic religion, it never overcomes its subjective character, remaining always a religion *for the sake of man*. Men are religious in order to conjure the spirits hovering behind the veil of Nature, to free themselves from the oppressive sway of the cosmos. It matters not whether the Llama priest confines the evil spirits in his jugs, whether the nature-gods of the Orient are invoked to afford shelter against the forces of nature, whether the loftier gods of Greece are worshipped in their ascendency above nature, or whether, finally, ideal-istic philosophy presents the spirit of man himself as the real object of adoration;—in all these different forms it is and remains a religion fostered for man's sake, aiming at his safety, his liberty, his elevation, and partly also at his triumph over death. And even when a religion of this kind has developed itself into monotheism, the god whom it worships, remains invariably a god who exists in order to help man, in order to secure good order and tranquillity for the State, to furnish assist- ance and deliverance in time of need, or to strengthen the nobler and higher impulse of the human heart in its ceaseless struggle with the degrading influences of sin. The consequence of this is that all such religion thrives in time of famine and pestilence, it flourishes among the poor and oppressed, and it expands among the humble and the feeble; but it pines away in the days of prosperity, it fails to attract the well-to-do, it is abandoned by those who are more highly cultured. As soon as the more civilized classes enjoy tranquillity and comfort, and by the progress of science feel more and more delivered from the pressure of the cosmos, they throw away the crutches of religion, and with a sneer at everything holy, go stumbling forward on their own poor legs. This is the fatal end of egoistic reli- gion;—it becomes superfluous and disappears as soon as the egoistic interests are satisfied. This was the course of religion among all non-Christian nations, in earlier times, and the same phenomenon is repeating itself in our own century, among nominal Christians of the higher, more properous and more cultured classes of society.

Now the position of Calvinism is diametrically opposed

to all this. It does not deny that religion has also its human and subjective side; it does not dispute the fact that religion is promoted, encouraged and strengthened by our disposition to seek help in time of need and spiritual elevation in the face of sensual passions; but it maintains that it reverses the proper order of things to seek, in these accidental motives, the *essence* and the very *purpose* of religion. The Calvinist values all of these as *fruits* which are produced by religion, or as props which give it support, but he refuses to honour them as the reason of its existence. Of course, religion, as such, produces *also* a blessing for man, but it does not exist for the sake of man. It is not God who exists for the sake of His creation;—the creation exists for the sake of God. For, as the Scripture says, He has created all things for Himself.

For this reason God even impressed a religious expression on the whole of unconscious nature,—on plants, on animals and also on children. "The whole earth is full of His glory." "How excellent is Thy Name, God, in all the earth." "The Heavens declare the glory of God and the firmament sheweth His handiwork." "Out of the mouths of babes and sucklings Thou hast ordained praise." Frost and hail, snow and vapour, the abyss and the hurricane,—everything does praise God. But just as the entire creation reaches its culminating point in man, so also religion finds its clear expression only in man who is made in the image of God, and this not because man seeks it, but because God Himself implanted in man's nature the real essential religious expression, by means of the "seed of religion" (*semen religionis*), as Calvin defines it, sown in our human heart.

God Himself *makes* man religious by means of the *sensus divinitatis*, i.e., the sense of the Divine, which He causes to strike the chords on the harp of his soul. A sound of need interrupts the pure harmony of this divine melody, but only in consequence of sin. In its original form, in its natural condition, religion is exclusively a sentiment of *admiration* and *adoration*, which elevates and unites, not a feeling of dependence which severs and depresses. Just as the anthem of the Seraphim around the throne is one uninterrupted cry of "*Holy,—Holy,—Holy*"!, so also the religion of man upon this earth should consist in one echoing of God's glory, as our Creator and Inspirer. The starting-point of every motive in religion is God and not Man. Man is the instrument and means, God alone is here the goal, the point of departure and the point of arrival, the fountain, from which the waters flow, and at the same time, the ocean into which they finally return. To be irreligious is to forsake the highest aim of our existence, and on the other hand to covet no other existence than for the sake of God, to long for nothing but for the will of God, and to be wholly absorbed in the glory of the name of the Lord, such is the pith and kernel of all true religion. "Hallowed be thy Name. Thy kingdom come. Thy Will be done," is the threefold petition, which gives utterance to all true religion. Our watchword must be,—"Seek first the kingdom of God," and after that, think of your own need. First stands the confession of the absolute sovereignty

of the Triune God; for of Him, through Him, and
unto Him are all things. And therefore our prayer
remains the deepest expression of all religious life. This
is the fundamental conception of religion as maintained
by Calvinism, and hitherto, no one has ever found a
higher conception. For no higher conception *can* be
found. The fundamental thought of Calvinism, at the
same time the fundamental thought of the Bible, and of .
Christianity itself, leads, in the domain of religion to the
realization of the highest ideal. Nor has the philosophy
of religion in our own century, in its most daring flights,
ever attained a higher point of view nor a more ideal
conception.

The second principal question in all religion is whether
it must be *direct*, or *mediate*. Must there stand a church,
a priest, or, as of old, a sorcerer, a dispenser of sacred
mysteries, between God and the soul, or shall all intervening links be cast away, so that the bond of religion
shall bind the soul directly to God. Now we find that
in all non-Christian religions, without any exception,
human intercessors are deemed necessary, and in the
domain of Christianity itself the intercessor intruded
again upon the scene, in the Blessed Virgin, in the host
of angels, in the saints and martyrs, and in the priestly
hierarchy of the clergy; and although Luther took the
field against all priestly mediation, yet the church which
is called by his name, renewed by its title of "*ecclesia
docens*" the office of mediator and steward of mysteries.
On this point also it was Calvin, and he alone, who

attained to the full realization of the ideal of pure spiritual religion. Religion, as he conceived it, must *"nullis mediis interpositis"*, i.e., without any creaturely interces- sion, realize the direct communion between God and the human heart. Not because of any hatred against priests, as such, not because of any undervaluing of the martyrs, nor underestimating the significance of angels, but solely because Calvin felt bound to vindicate the essence of religion and the glory of God in that essence, and abso- lutely devoid of all yielding or wavering, he waged war, with holy indignation, against everything that interposed itself between the soul and God. Of course he clearly perceived that in order to be fitted for the true religion, fallen man needs a Mediator, but such a mediator could not be found in any fellow-man. Only the God-man,— only God Himself could be such a mediator. And this mediatorship could be confirmed not by us, but only from the side of God, by the indwelling of God the Holy Spirit in the heart of the regenerated.

In all religion God Himself must be the active power. He must *make* us religious, He must *give* us the religious disposition, nothing being left to us but the power to give form and expression to the deep religious sentiment wich He, Himself, stirred in the depth of our heart. There we see the mistake of those who regarded Calvin as only an *Augustinus redivivus.* Notwithstand- ing his sublime confession of God's holy grace, Au- gustine remained *the Bishop.* He kept his intermediate position between the Triune God and the layman. And although prominent among the most pious men of his time, he had so little insight into the real claims of thorough-going religion on behalf of laymen that in his dogmatics he lauds the church as the mystical Purveyor, into whose bosom God caused all grace to flow and from whose treasure all men had to accept it. Only he, therefore, who superficially confines his attention to predestination can confuse Augustinianism and Calvinism. Religion *for the sake of man* carries with it the position that man has to act as a mediator for his fellow-man. Religion *for the sake of God* inexorably excludes every human mediatorship. As long as it remains the chief purpose of religion to help man, and as long as man is understood to deserve grace by his devotion, it is perfectly natural that the man of inferior piety should invoke the mediation of the holier man. Another must procure for him what he cannot procure for himself. The fruit on the branches hangs too high, and, therefore, the higher-reaching man has to pluck it, and hand it down to his helpless comrade. If, on the contrary, the demand of religion is that *every* human heart must give glory to God, no man can appear before God on behalf of another. Then every single human being must appear personally, for himself, and religion achieves its aim only in the *general priesthood of believers.* Even the new-born babe must have received the seed of religion from God Himself; and in case it dies without being baptized, it must not be sent off to a *limbus innocentium*, but, if elected, enter, even as the long-lived, into personal communion with God, for all eternity.

The importance of this second point, in the question of religion, culminating, as it does, in the confession of personal election, is incalculable. On the one hand, all religion must tend *to make man free*, that by a clear utterance he may express that general religious impression stamped, by God Himself, upon unconscious nature. On the other hand, every appearance of an interposing priest or enchanter in the domain of religion fetters the human spirit, in a chain which presses the more woefully the more the piety increases in fervour. In the Church of Rome, even at the present day, the *bons catholiques* are most closely confined in the fetters of the clerus. Only the Roman-Catholic whose piety has decreased, is able to secure for himself a partial liberty by loosening more than half way the tie which connects him with his church. In the Lutheran churches the clerical fetters are less confining, yet far from being loosened, entirely. And only in churches which take their stand in Calvinism, do we find that spiritual independence which enables the believer to oppose, if need be, and for God's sake, even the most powerful officebearer in his church. Only he who personally stands before God on his own account, and enjoys an uninterrupted communion with God, can properly display the glorious wings of liberty. And both in Holland and in France, in England as well as in America, the historic result affords most undeniable evidence of the fact that despotism has found no more invincible antagonists, and liberty of conscience no braver, no more resolute champions than the followers of Calvin. In the last analysis, the cause of this phenomenon lies in the fact that the effect of every clerical interposition invariably was, and must be, to make religion external and to smother it with sacerdotal forms. Only where all priestly inter-

vention disappears, where God's sovereign election from
all eternity binds the inward soul directly to God Himself,
and where the ray of divine light enters straightway
into the depth of our heart,—only there does religion,
in its most absolute sense, gain its ideal realization.

This leads me, naturally, to the third religious
question: Is religion *partial*, or is it all-subduing, and
comprehensive,—*universal* in the strict sense of the word?
Now, if the aim of religion be found in man himself
and if its realization be made dependent on clerical media-
tors, religion cannot be but *partial*. In that case it
follows logically that every man confines his religion
to those occurrences of his life by which his religious
needs are stirred, and to those cases in which he finds
human intervention at his disposal. The partial character
of this sort of religion shows itself in three particulars:
in the religious *organ* through which, in the *sphere* in
which, and in the *group of persons* among which, religion
has to thrive and flourish.

Recent controversy affords a pertinent illustration of
the first limitation. The wise men of our generation
maintain that religion has to retire from the precinct
of the human intellect. It must seek to express itself
either by means of the mystical feelings, or else by
means of the practical will. Mystical and ethical in-
clinations are hailed with enthusiasm, in the domain
of religion, but in that same domain the intellect, as
leading to metaphysical hallucinations, must be muzzled.
Metaphysics and Dogmatics are increasingly tabooed,

and Agnosticism is ever more loudly acclaimed as the
solution of the great enigma. On the rivers of sentiment
and of feeling, navigation is made duty-free, and ethical
activity is becoming the only touch-stone for testing
the religious gold; but Metaphysics is avoided as
drowning us in a swamp. Whatsoever announces itself
with the pretension of an axiomatic dogma, is rejected
as irreligious contraband. And although that same
Christ whom these very scholars honour as a religious
genius has taught us most emphatically: "Thou shalt
love God, not only with all thy heart and with all thy
strength, but also *with all thy mind*", yet they, on the
contrary, venture to dismiss our mind, or intellect, as
unfit for use, in this holy domain, and as not fulfilling
the requirements of a religious organ.

Thus the religious organ being found, not in the whole
of our being, but in part of it, being confined to our feelings
and our will, consequently also *the sphere* of religious life
also must assume in consequence the same *partial character*. Religion is excluded from science, and its authority
from the domain of public life; henceforth the inner chamber, the cell for prayer, and the secrecy of the heart should
be its exclusive dwelling place. By his *du sollst*, Kant
limited the sphere of religion to the ethical life. The
mystics of our own times banish religion to the retreats
of sentiment. And the result is that, in many different
ways, religion, once the central force of human life, is
now placed alongside of it; and, far from the thriving
of the world, is understood to hide itself in a distant
and almost private retreat.

This brings us naturally to the third characteristic

note of this partial view of religion;—religion as per-
taining not to all, but only to *the group of pious people*
among our generation. Thus the limitation of the *organ*
of religion brings about the limitation of its *sphere*, and
the limitation of its sphere consequently brings about
the limitation of its group or *circle* among men. Just
as art is understood to have an *organ* of its own, a
sphere of its own, and therefore, also, its own *circle* of
devotees, so also, according to this view, must it be
with religion. It so happens that the great bulk of the
people are almost devoid of mystical feeling, and energetic
strength of will. For this reason they have either no
perception of the glow of mysticism, or are incapable of
really pious deeds. But there are also those whose inner
life is overflowing with a sense of the Infinite, or who
are full of holy energy, and among such it is that
piety and religion flourish most brilliantly both in their
imaginative power, and in their realizing capability.

From a quite different standpoint, Rome gradually
and increasingly came to favour the same partial views.
She knew religion only as it existed in her own church,
and considered the influence of religion to be confined
to that portion of life which she had consecrated. I fully
acknowledge that she tried to draw all human life as
far as possible into the holy sphere, but everything
outside this sphere, everything not touched by baptism,
nor aspersed by her holy water, was devoid of all
genuine religious efficiency. And just as Rome drew a
boundary line between the consecrated and the profane
sides of life, she also subdivided her own sacred precincts
according to different degrees of religious intensity;—

the clergy and the cloister constituting the *Holy of Holies*, the pious laity forming the *Holy Place*, thus leaving the *Outer Court* to those who, although baptized, continued to prefer to church-devotion the often sinful pleasures of the world;—a system of limitation and division, which for those in the *Outer Court*, ended in setting nine tenths of practical life outside of all religion. So religion was made partial, by carrying it from ordinary days to days of festival, from days of prosperity to times of danger and sickness, and from the fulness of life to the time of approaching death. A dualistic system which has found its most emphatic expression in the praxis of the Carnival, giving Religion a full sway over the soul during the weeks of Lent, but leaving to the flesh a fair chance, before descending into this vale of gloom, to empty to the dregs the full cup of pleasure, if not of mirth and folly.

Now this whole view of the matter is squarely antagonized by Calvinism, which vindicates for religion its full universal character, and its complete universal application. If everything that is, exists for the sake of God, then it follows that the whole creation must give glory to God. The sun, moon, and stars in the firmament, the birds of the air, the whole of Nature around us, but, above all, man himself, who, priestlike, must consecrate to God the whole of creation, and all life thriving in it. And although sin has deadened a large part of creation to the glory of God, the demand,—the ideal, remains unchangeable, that *every* creature must be immersed in the stream of religion, and end by lying as a religious offering on the altar of the Almighty.

A religion confined to feeling or will is therefore unthink-
able to the Calvinist. The sacred anointing of the
priest of creation must reach down to his beard and
to the hem of his garment. His whole being, including
all his abilities and powers, must be pervaded by the
sensus divinitatis, and how then could he exclude his
rational consciousness,—the λόγος which is in him,—the
light of thought which comes from God Himself to
irradiate him? To possess his God for the underground
world of his feelings, and in the outworks of the exertion
of his will, but not in his inner self,* in the very
centre of his consciousness, and his thought; to have
fixed starting-points for the study of nature and
axiomatic strongholds for practical life, but to have no
fixed support in his thoughts about the Creator Himself,—
all of this was, for the Calvinist, the very denying of
the Eternal Logos.

The same character of universality was claimed by
the Calvinist for the *sphere* of religion and its *circle*
of influence among men. Everything that has been created
was, in its creation, furnished by God with an unchangeable law of its existence. And because God has fully
ordained such laws and ordinances for all life, therefore
the Calvinist demands that all life be consecrated to His
service, in strict obedience. A religion confined to the
closet, the cell, or the church, therefore, Calvin abhors.
With the Psalmist, he calls upon heaven and earth, he
calls upon all peoples and nations to give glory to God.
God is present in all life, with the influence of His
omnipresent and almighty power, and no sphere of
human life is conceivable in wich religion does not

maintain its demands that God shall be praised, that God's ordinances shall be observed, and that every *labora* shall be permeated with its *ora* in fervent and ceaseless prayer. Wherever man may stand, whatever he may do, to whatever he may apply his hand, in agriculture, in commerce, and in industry, or his mind, in the world of art, and science, he is, in whatsoever it may be, constantly standing before the face of his God, he is employed in the service of his God, he has strictly to obey his God, and above all, he has to aim at the glory of his God.—Consequently, it is impossible for a Calvinist to confine religion to a single group, or to some circles among men. Religion concerns the whole of our human race. This race is the product of God's creation. It is His wonderful workmanship, His absolute possession. Therefore the whole of mankind must be imbued with the fear of God,—old as well as young,—low as well as high,—not only those who have become initiated into His mysteries, but also those who still stand afar off. For not only did God create all men, not only is He all for all men, but His grace also extends itself, not only as a special grace, to the elect, but also as a common grace (gratia communis), to all mankind. To be sure there is a concentration of religious light and life in the Church, but then in the walls of this church, there are wide open windows, and through these spacious windows the light of the Eternal has to radiate over the whole world. Here is a city, set upon a hill, which every man can see afar of. Here is a holy salt that penetrates in every direction, checking all corruption. And even he who does not yet imbibe

the higher light, or maybe shuts his eyes to it, is
nevertheless admonished, with equal emphasis, and in
all things, to give glory to the name of the Lord.
All partial religion drives the wedge of dualism into
life, but the true Calvinist never forsakes the standard
of religious monism. One supreme calling must impress
the stamp of *one-ness* upon *all* human life, because one
God upholds and preserves it, just as He created it all.

This brings us, without any further transition, to
our fourth main question, *viz.*, Must religion be *normal,*
or abnormal, i e., *soteriological?* The distinction which
I have in mind here is concerned with the question,
whether in the matter of religion we must reckon *de
facto* with man in his present condition as *normal,* or
as having fallen into sin, and having therefore become
abnormal. In the latter case religion must necessarily
assume a soteriological character. Now the prevailing
idea, at present, favours the view that religion has to
start from man as being *normal.* Not of course as
though our race as a whole should conform already
to the highest religious norm. This nobody affirms.
Everyone knows better than to make such an absurd
statement. As a matter of fact, we meet with much
irreligiousness, and imperfect religious development continues to be the rule. But precisely in this slow and
gradual progress from the lowest forms to the highest
ideals, the development demanded by this normal view
of religion contends that it has found confirmation.
According to this view, the first traces of religion are

found in animals. They are seen in the dog who adores his master, and as the *homo sapiens* developes out of the chimpanzee, so religion only enters upon a higher stage. Since that time religion has passed through all the notes of the gamut. At present it is engaged in loosening itself from the bands of Church and dogma, to pass on to what is again considered a higher stage, namely, *the unconscious feeling for the Unknown Infinite.*—Now, this whole theory is opposed by that other and entirely different theory, which, without denying the preformation of so much that is human, in the animal, or the fact that (if you will allow me to say so) animals were created after the image of man, just as man was created after the image of God, nevertheless maintains that the first man was created in perfect relations to his God, *i.e.*, as imbued by a pure and genuine religion, and consequently explains the many low, imperfect and absurd forms of religion found in Paganism, not as the result of his creation but as the outcome of his Fall. These low and imperfect forms of religion are not to be understood as a process that leads from a lower to a higher, but as a lamentable degeneration,—a degeneration, which, in the nature of the case, makes the restoration of the true religion possible only in the soteriological way. Now in the choice between these two theories Calvinism allows no hesitation. Standing himself, with this question, too, before the face of God, the Calvinist was so impressed with the holiness of God that the consciousness of guilt immediately lacerated his soul, and the terrible nature of sin pressed on his heart as with an intolerable

weight Every attempt to explain sin, as an incomplete
stage on the way to perfection, aroused his wrath, as
an insult to the majesty of God. He confessed, from
the beginning, the same truth which Buckle has demonstrated empirically in his "History of Civilization in
England", *viz.*, that the *forms* in which sin makes its
appearance may show us a gradual refinement, but that
the moral condition of the human heart, as such, has·
remained the same throughout all the centuries. To the
de profundis with which, thirty centuries ago, the soul
of David cried unto God, the troubled soul of every
child of God in the sixteenth century still sounded a
response with undiminished power. The conception of
the corruption of sin as the source of all human misery
was nowhere more profound than in Calvin's environment. Even in the assertions which the Calvinist made,
in accordance with Holy Scripture, concerning hell and
damnation, there is no coarseness, no rudeness, but only
that clearness which is the result of the utmost seriousness
of life, and the undaunted courage of a deep-rooted
conviction of the holiness of the most High. Did not
He, from whose lips flowed the most tender, and the
most winning words,—did not He, Himself also speak
most decidedly and repeatedly of an "outer darkness",
of a "fire that cannot be quenched", and of a "worm
that dieth not"? And in this, also, Calvin was right,
for to refuse to assent to these words is nothing but a
lack of thoroughgoing consistency. It shews a want of
sincerity in our confession of the holiness of God, and
of the destructive power of sin. And on the contrary,
in this spiritual experience of sin, in this empirical con-

sideration of the misery of life, in this lofty impression
of the holiness of God, and in this staunchness of his
convictions, which led him to follow his conclusions to
the bitter end, the Calvinist found the roots of the
necessity first of *Regeneration*, for real *existence*, and
secondly, the necessity of *Revelation*, for clear *consciousness*.

Now, my subject does not induce me to speak in
detail of regeneration, as that immediate act by which
God, as it were, sets right again the crooked wheel of
life. But it is necessary that I say a few words concerning
Revelation, and the authority of the Holy Scriptures.
Very improperly, the Scriptures have been represented,
by Schweizer and others, as only the *formal* principle
of the Reformed confession. The conception of genuine
Calvinism lies much deeper. The meaning of Calvin was
expressed in what he called the *necessitas S. Scripturae*;
i. e. the need of Scriptural revelation. This *necessitas
S. S.* was for Calvin the unavoidable expression for the
all-dominating authority of the Holy Scriptures, and even
now it is this very dogma which enables us to understand, why it is that the Calvinist of to-day considers
the critical analysis and the application of the critical
solvent to the Scriptures as tantamount to an abandoning
of Christianity itself. In Paradise, before the Fall, there
was no Bible, and there will be no Bible in the future
Paradise of glory. When the transparent light, kindled
by Nature, addresses us directly, and the inner word of
God sounds in our heart in its original clearness, and
all human words are sincere, and the function of our
inner ear is perfectly performed, why should we need a

Bible? What mother loses herself in a treatise upon the
"love of our children" the very moment that her own
dear ones are playing about her knee, and God allows
her to drink in their love with full draughts? But, in
our present condition, this immediate communion with
God by means of nature, and of our own heart is lost.
Sin brought separation instead, and the opposition which
is manifest nowadays, against the authority of the Holy .
Scriptures is based on nothing else than the false supposition that, our condition being still normal, our religion
need not be soteriological. For of course, in that case,
the Bible is not wanted, it becomes, indeed, a hindrance,
and grates upon your feelings, since it interposes a book
between God and your heart. Oral communication excludes writing. When the sun shines in your house,
bright and clear, you turn off the electric light, but
when the sun disappears, below the horizon, you feel
the *necessitas luminis artificiosi, i. e.*, the need of artificial
light, and the artificial light is kindled in every dwelling.
Now this is the case in matters of religion. When there
are no mists to hide the majesty of the divine light
from our eyes, what need is there then for a lamp
unto the feet, or a light upon the path? But when
history, experience and consciousness all unite in stating
the fact that the pure and full light of Heaven *has*
disappeared, and that we are groping about in the dark,
then, a different, or if you will, an artificial light *must*
be kindled for us;—and such a light God has kindled
for us in His Holy Word.

For the Calvinist, therefore, the necessity of the Holy
Scriptures does not rest in ratiocination, but on the

immediate testimony of the Holy Spirit,—on the *testimonium spiritus Sancti*. Our theory of inspiration is the product of historical deduction, and so is also every canonical declaration of the Scriptures. But the magnetic power with which the Scripture influences the soul, and draws it to itself, just as the magnet draws the steel, is not derived, but immediate. All of this takes place in a manner, which is not magical, nor unfathomably mystical, but clear, and easy to be understood. God regenerates us,—that is to say he rekindles in our heart the lamp sin had blown out. The necessary consequence of this regeneration is an irreconcilable conflict between the inner world of our heart and the world outside, and this conflict is ever the more intensified the more the regenerative principle pervades our consiousness. Now, in the Bible, God reveals, to the regenerate, a world of thought, a world of energies, a world of full and beautiful life, which stands in direct opposition to his ordinary world, but which proves to agree in a wonderful way with the new life that has sprung up in his heart. So the regenerate begins to guess the identity of what is stirring in the depth of his own soul, and of what is revealed to him in Scripture, thereby learning both the inanity of the world around him, and the divine reality of the world of the Scriptures, and as soon as this has become a certainty to him, he has personally received the *testimony* of the *Holy Spirit*. Everything that is in him thirsted for the Father of all Lights and Spirits. Outside the Scripture, he discovered only vague shadows. But now as he looks upward, through the prism of the Scriptures, he rediscovers his Father and his God.—For this reason he puts no shackles on science. If a man wants to criticise, let him criticise. Such criticism even holds the promise that it will deepen our own insight into the structure of the scriptural edifice. Only no Calvinist ever allows the critic to dash out of his hand, for a moment, the *prism itself* which breaks up the divine ray of light into its brilliant tints and colours. No appeal to the grace bestowed inwardly, no pointing to the fruits of the Holy Ghost, can enable him to dispense with the *necessitas* which the soteriological standpoint of religion among sinners carries with it. As mere *entities* we share our life with plants and animals. *Unconscious* life we share with the children, and with the sleeping man, and even with the man who has lost his reason. That which distinguishes us, as higher beings, and as wide awake men, is our *full self-consciousness*, and therefore, if religion, as the highest vital function, is to operate also in that highest sphere of self-consciousness, it must follow that soteriological religion, next to the *necessitas* of inward *palingenesis*, demands also the *necessitas* of an assistant light, of revelation to be kindled in our twilight. And this assistant light coming from God Himself, but handed to us by human agency, beams upon us in His holy Word.

Summing up the results of our investigations thus far, I may express my conclusion as follows. In each one of the four great problems of religion, Calvinism has expressed its conviction in an appropriate dogma, and each time has made that choice which even now, after three centuries, satisfies the most ideal wants, and leaves the way open for an ever richer development.

First, it regards religion, not in an utilitarian, or eudæmonistic sense, as existing for the sake of man, but for God, and for God alone. This is its dogma of *God's souvereignty*. *Secondly*, in religion there must be no intermediation of any creature between God and the soul;—all religion is the immediate work of God Himself, in the inner heart. This is the doctrine of *Election*. *Thirdly*, religion is not partial but universal;—this is the dogma of *common or universal grace*. And, finally, in our sinful condition, religion cannot be normal, but has to be *soteriological;*—this is its position in the twofold dogma of the necessity of Regeneration, and of the *necessitas S. Scripturae*.

Having considered Religion as such, and coming now *to the Church*, as its organized form, or its phenomenal appearance, I shall present, in three successive stages, the Calvinistic conception of the *essence*, the *manifestation* and the *purpose* of the Church of Christ upon earth.

In its essence, for the Calvinist, the Church is a spiritual organism, including heaven and earth, but having at present, its centre, and the starting-point for its action, not upon earth, but in heaven. This is to be understood thus: God created the Cosmos geocentrically, i. e., He placed the spiritual centre of this Cosmos on our planet, and caused all the divisions of the kingdoms of nature, on this earth, to culminate in man, upon whom, as the bearer of His image He called to consecrate the Cosmos to His glory. In God's creation, therefore, man stands as the prophet, priest and king, and although sin has disturbed these high designs, yet God pushes them onward. He so loves His world that He has given Himself to it, in the person of His Son, and thus He has again brought our race, and through our race, His whole Cosmos, into a renewed contact with eternal life. To be sure, many branches and leaves fell off the tree of the human race, yet the tree itself shall be saved; on its new root in Christ, it shall once more blossom gloriously. For regeneration does not save a few isolated individuals, finally to be joined together mechanically as an aggregate heap. Regeneration saves the organism, itself, of our race. And therefore all regenerate human life, forms one organic body, of which Christ is the Head, and whose members are bound together by their mystical union with Him. But not before the second Advent, shall this new all-embracing organism manifest itself as the centre of the cosmos. At present it is hidden. Here, on earth it is only as it were its silhouette that can be dimly discerned. In the Future, *this new Jerusalem* shall descend from God, out of heaven, but at present it withdraws its beams from our sight in the mysteries of the invisible. And therefore the true sanctuary is now *above*. On high are both the Altar of Atonement, and the incense-Altar of Prayer; and on high is Christ, as the only priest who, according to Melchizedek's ordinance, ministers at the Altar, in the sanctuary, before God.

Now, in the middle ages, the Church had more and more lost sight of this celestial character;—she had become worldly in her nature. The Sanctuary was again brought back to earth, the altar was rebuilt of stone, and a priestly hierarchy had reconstituted itself for the ministrations of the altar. Next of course it was necessary also to renew the tangible sacrifice on earth, and this at last brought the church to create the unbloody offering of the Mass. Now against all this, Calvinism opposed itself, not to contend against priesthood on principle, or against altars as such, or against sacrifice in itself, because the office of priest cannot perish, and everyone knowing the fact of sin realizes in his own heart, the absolute need of a propitiatory sacrifice; but in order to do away with all this worldly paraphernalia, and to call believers to lift up their eyes again, on high, to the real sanctuary, where Christ, our only priest, ministers at the only real altar. The battle was waged, not against *sacerdotium*, but against *sacerdotalism*, and Calvin alone fought this battle through to the end, with thorough consistency. Lutherans and Episcopalians *rebuilt* a kind of altar, on earth; Calvinism alone dared to put it away, entirely. Consequently, among the Episcopalians, the earthly priesthood was retained, even in the form* of a hierarchy; in Lutheran lands the sovereign became *summus episcopus* and the divisions of ecclesiastical ranks were imitated; but Calvinism proclaimed the absolute equality of all who engaged in the service of the church, and refused to ascribe to its leaders and officebearers any other character than that of *Ministers, (i.e., servants.)* That which, under the shadows of the Old Testament dispensation, furnished intuitive instruction by types and symbols, now that the types were fulfilled, had become to Calvin, a detriment

to the glory of Christ, and lowered the heavenly nature
of the Church. Therefore, Calvinism could not rest
until this worldly tinsel had ceased to charm and attract
the eye. Only when the last grain of the sacerdotal
leaven had been eliminated, could the Church on earth
again become the outer court, from which believers
could look up and onward to the real sanctuary of the
living God in heaven.

The Westminster Confession beautifully sets forth this
heavenly all-embracing nature of the Church, when it
says:—"The Catholic or Universal Church, which is
invisible, consists of the whole number of the elect
that have been, are or shall be, gathered into one,
under Christ the Head, thereof; and is the spouse, the
body, the fulness of Him that filleth all in all." Only
thus was the dogma of the invisible church religiously
consecrated and apprehended in its cosmological, and
enduring significance. For, of course, the reality and
fulness of the Church of Christ cannot exist on earth.
Here is found, at most, one generation of believers at
a time, in the portal of the Temple;—all previous
generations, from the beginning and foundation of the
world, had left this earth, and had gone up on high.
Therefore, those who remained here, were, *eo ipso*, *pil-
grims*, meaning thereby that they were marching from
the portal unto the Sanctuary itself, no possibility of
salvation after death remaining for those who had not
been united to Christ, during this present life. No room
could be left for masses for the dead, nor for a call
to repentance on the other side of the grave, as German
Theologians are now advocating. For all such proces-

sional, and gradual transitions, were regarded by Calvin
as destroying the absolute contrast between the essence
of the Church in Heaven, and its imperfect form, here
on earth. The church on earth does not send *up* its
light to heaven, but the Church in heaven must send
its light *down* to the Church on earth. There is now,
as it were, a curtain stretched, before the eye, which
hinders it from penetrating while on earth, into the real
essence of the Church. Therefore, all that remains possible
to us on earth is first, a mystical communion with that
real Church, by means of the Spirit, and in the second
place the enjoyment of the shadows which are displaying
themselves on the transparent curtain before us. Accordingly, no child of God should imagine that the real
Church is here on earth, and that behind the curtain
there is only an ideal product of our imagination; but,
on the contrary, he has to confess that Christ in human
form, in our flesh, has entered into the invisible, behind
the curtain; and that, with Him, around Him, and in
Him, our Head, is the real church, the real and essential
sanctuary of our salvation.

After having thus clearly grasped the nature of the
Church, in its bearing upon the re-creation both of
our human race and of the Cosmos as a whole, let us
now turn our attention to its *form of manifestation*,
here on earth. As such it displays, unto us, different
local congregations of believers, groups of *confessors*,
living in some ecclesiastical union, in obedience to the
ordinances of Christ Himself. The Church on earth

is not an institution for the dispensation of grace, as if it were a dispensary of spiritual medicines. There is no mystical, spiritual order, gifted with mystical, powers to operate with a magical influence upon laymen. There are only *regenerated and confessing individuals*, who, in accordance with the Scriptural command, and under the influence of the sociological element of all religion, have formed a society, and are endeavouring to live together in subordination to Christ as their king. This, alone, is the church on earth,—not the building,—not the institution,—not a spiritual order. For Calvin, the Church is found in the *confessing individuals them-selves*,—not in each individual separately, but in all of them taken together, and united, not as they themselves see fit, but according to the ordinances of Christ. In the church on earth, the universal priesthood of believers must be realized. Do not misunderstand me. I do not say: The Church consists of pious persons united in groups for religious purposes. That, in itself, would have nothing in common with the church. The real, heavenly, invisible church must manifest itself *in* the earthly church. If not, you will have a society, but no church. Now the real, essential church is and remains the body of Christ, of which regenerate persons are members. Therefore the Church on earth consists only of those who have been incorporated into Christ, who bow before Him, live in His Word, and adhere to His ordinances; and for this reason the church on earth has to preach the Word, to administer the sacraments, and to exercise discipline, and in everything to stand before the face of God.

This at the same time determines the form of government of this church on earth. This government,
like the church itself, originates in Heaven, in Christ.
He most effectually rules, governs His church by means
of the Holy Spirit, by whom He works in His members.
Therefore, all being equal under Him, there can be no
distinctions of rank among believers; there are only
ministers, who serve, lead and regulate; a thoroughly
Presbyterian form of government; the Church power
descending directly from Christ Himself, into the congregation, concentrated from the congregation in the
ministers, and by them being administered unto the
brethren. So the sovereignty of Christ remains absolutely monarchical, but the government of the Church
on earth becomes democratic to its bones and marrow;
a system leading logically to this other sequence, that
all believers and all congregations being of an equal
standing, no Church may exercise any dominion over
another, but that all local churches are of equal rank,
and as manifestations of one and the same body, can
only be united synodically, i.e., by way of *confederation*.

Now let me draw your attention to another most
important consequence of this same principle, *viz.*, to
the multiformity of denominations as the necessary result
of the differentiation of the churches, according to the
different degrees of their purity. If the church is
considered to be an institute of grace, independent of
the believers, or an institute in which a hierarchical
priesthood distributes the treasury of grace entrusted
to it, the result must be that this hierarchy itself
extends through all nations, and imparts the same stamp

to all forms of ecclesiastical life. But if the church consists in the *congregation of believers*, if the churches are formed by the union of confessors, and are united only in the way of confederation, then the differences of climate and of nation, of historical past, and of disposition of mind come in to exercise a widely varie-gating influence, and multiformity in ecclesiastical matters must be the result. A result, therefore, of very far- . reaching importance, because it annihilates the absolute character of every visible Church, and places them all side by side, as differing in degrees of purity, but always remaining in some way or other a manifestation of one holy and catholic church of Christ in Heaven.

I do not say that Calvinistic theologians have pro-claimed this full consequence from the beginning. The desire for ruling power lurked also at the door of their heart, and even apart from this dangerous disposition it was right and natural for them theoretically to judge each church according to the standard of their own ideals. But this does not in the least detract from the great significance of the fact that by regarding their church, not as a hierarchy or institution, but as the gathering of individual confessors, they started for the life of the church, as well as for the life of the state, and civil society, from the principle not of compulsion, but of liberty. For, of course by virtue of this starting-point there was no other church-power superior to the local churches, save only what the churches themselves constituted, by means of their confederation. Hence it followed of necessity that the natural and historic dif-ferences between men should also, wedge-like, force their

way into the phenomenal life of the church upon earth.
National differences of morals, differences of disposition
and of emotions, different degrees in depth of life and
insight, necessarily resulted in emphasizing first one,
and then another side of the same truth. Hence the
numerous sects and denominations into which the
external church-life has fallen by virtue of this principle.
So on our side there are denominations which may
have departed from the rich deep and full Calvinistic
Confession, in no small degree, even such as bitterly
oppose more than one capital article of our confession;
yet they all owe their origin to a deep-rooted opposition to sacerdotalism, and to the acknowledgment of
the church as the "congregation of believers", the truth
in which Calvinism expressed its fundamental conception.
And although this fact unavoidably led to much unholy
rivalry, and even to sinful errors of conduct; yet, after
an experience of three centuries it must be confessed
that this multiformity, which is inseparably connected
with the fundamental thought of Calvinism, has been
much more favourable to the growth and prosperity of
religious life than the compulsory uniformity in which
others sought the very basis of its strength. And fruit
is to be expected more abundantly still in the future,
provided only that the principle of ecclesiastical liberty
does not degenerate into indifference, and that no church,
which, in its name and confession still upholds the
Calvinistic banner, omits to fulfil its holy mission of
recommending to others the superiority of its principles.
. Still another point must be brought forward in this
connection. The conception of the Church as the "con-

gregation of believers" might lead to the conception
that it included the believers only, without their children.
This, however, is by no means the teaching of Calvinism;
its teching on the subject of infant baptism showing
quite the contrary. Believers who meet together do not
thereby sever the natural bond that binds them to their
offspring. On the contrary, they consecrate this bond,
and by baptism incorporate their children in the communion of their church, and these minors are kept in
this Church communion until, when of age, they become
themselves confessors, or sever themselves from the
church by their unbelief. This is the all-important Calvinistic dogma of the *Covenant;* a prominent article
of our confession, showing that the waters of the Church
do not flow outside the natural stream of human life,
but cause the life of the church to proceed hand in
hand with the natural organic reproduction of mankind
in its succeeding generations. *Covenant* and Church are
inseparable,—the covenant binding the church to the
race, and God Himself sealing in it the connection
between the life of grace, and the life of nature. Of
course Church discipline must come in here, in order to
preserve the purity of this Covenant as soon as the
intenpermeation of grace by nature tends to lower the
purity of the Church. From the Calvinistic point of
view, therefore, it is impossible to speak of a national
Church, as being destined to embrace all the inhabitants
of a whole country. A national Church, i.e., a church
comprising only one nation, and that nation entirely,
is a Heathen, or at most, a Jewish conception. The
Church of Christ is not national but ecumenical. Not

one single state, but the whole world is its domain. And when the Lutheran Reformers at the instigation of their sovereigns, nationalized their churches, and Calvinistic churches allowed themselves to deviate into the same track, they did not ascend to a higher conception than that of Rome's world-church, but descended to distinctly lower ground. Happily I may conclude by bearing witness that both our Synod of Dordt, and your not less venerable Westminster Assembly, have honoured again the ecumenical character of our Reformed Churches, thereby censuring as unpardonable, every deviation from the only right principle.

———————

Having thus far given an outline of the *nature* of the Church, and the *form* of its *manifestation*, let me now draw your attention in the last place to the *purpose* of its appearance on earth. I shall not say anything for the present on the separation of Church and State. This will naturally find place in the next Lecture. At present, I confine myself to the *purpose* that has been assigned to the Church in its pilgrimage through the world. That purpose cannot be human or egoistic, *to prepare the believer for Heaven*. A regenerate child, dying in the cradle, goes straight to Heaven, without any further preparation and wheresoever the Holy Ghost has kindled the spark of Eternal life in the soul, the perseverance of the saints assures the certainty of eternal salvation. Nay, upon earth also, the Church exists merely *for the sake of God*. Regeneration is sufficient for the elect man, to make him sure of his eternal

6

destiny, but it is not enough to satisfy the glory of
God in His work among men. For the glory of our
God it is necessary to have regeneration followed by
conversion, and to this conversion the Church must
contribute, by means of the preaching of the Word.
In the regenerate man glows the spark, but only in the
converted man does the spark burst into a blaze, and
that blaze radiates the light from the church into the.
world, that, according to our Lord's commandment,
our Father, which is in Heaven, may be glorified.
And both our conversion and our sanctification in good
works are only then marked by the lofty character
which Jesus demands, when we make them serve, in the
first place, not as the guarantee of our own salvation,
but rather the glorifying of God. In the second place,
the Church must fan this blaze, and make it brighten,
by the communion of the saints and by the Sacraments.
Only when hundreds of candles are burning from one
candelabrum, can the full brightness of the soft candle-
light strike us, and in the same way it is the communion of saints which has to unite the many small lights
of the single believers so that they may mutually
increase their brightness, and Christ, walking in the
midst of the seven candlesticks, may sacramentally
purify the glow of their brightness to a still more
brilliant fervour. Thus the purpose of the Church does
not lie in us, but in God, and in the glory of His name.

From this solemn purpose originates, in the same
way, the severely spiritual cultus which Calvinism tried
to restore in the services of the Church. Even Von
Hartman, the far-from-Christian philosopher, perceived

that cultus becomes more religious just in proportion as it has the courage to despise all external show, and the energy to evolve itself from symbolism, in order to clothe itself in beauty of a much higher order,—*the inward, spiritual beauty of the worshipping soul.* Sensual church services tend to soothe and flatter *man* religiously, and only the purely spiritual service of Calvinism aims at the .pure worship of God, and at adoration of Him in spirit and in truth.—The same tendency leads our church discipline, that indispensable element of every genuine Calvinistic church activity. Church discipline was also instituted in the first place, not to prevent scandals, nor even primilarily to prune the wild branches, but rather *to preserve the sanctity of the Covenant of God*, and ever to impress upon the outside world the solemn fact that God is too pure to look upon evil.— Finally we have the service of Church *philanthropy*, in the Diaconate which Calvin alone understood, and restored to its primordial honour. Neither Rome nor the Greek Church, neither the Lutheran nor the Epis-copal Church, caught the real meaning of the Diaconate. Calvinism alone has restored the Diaconate to its place of honour, as an indispensable and constitutive element of ecclesiastical life. But, in this Diaconate, also, the lofty principle must prevail that it may not glorify those who give alms, but only the name of Him who moves the hearts of the people to liberality. The Deacons are not *our* servants, but servants of Christ. That which we commit to them we simply give back to Christ, as stewards of what is His property; and in His name it must be distributed to His poor,—our brothers and sisters. The poor church-member, who thanks the Deacon and the giver, but not Christ, actually denies Him Who is the real and divine Giver, and Who through his deacons, purposes to make it manifest that for the whole man, and for the whole of life He is the *Christus Consolator*, the Heavenly Redeemer, anointed and appointed by God Himself, for our fallen race, from all eternity. And so, as you see, the result proves incontestably that in Calvinism, the fundamental conception of the *Church* fits perfectly to the fundamental idea of *Religion*. All egoism and eudæmonism are excluded from both, even unto the end. Always and ever we have a *Religion*, and a *Church*, for the sake of God, and not for the sake of man. The origin of the Church is in God, its form of manifestation is from God, and from beginning to end, its purpose is and remains *to magnify God's glory*.

Now finally, I come to the fruit of religion in our *practical life*, or the position taken by Calvinism in the *question of morals;*—the third and last division, with which this lecture on *Calvinism and Religion* will naturally conclude.

Here, the first thing that attracts our attention is the apparent contradiction between a confession, which, it is alleged, blunts the edge of moral incentives, and a practice, which, in moral earnestness exceeds the practice of all other religions. The Antinomian and the Puritan seemed to be mingled in this field like tares and wheat, so that at first sight it seemed as though the Antinomian were the logical result of the Calvinistic confession, and as though it were only by a fortunate inconsistency that the Puritan could infuse the warmth of his moral earnestness, into the all-congealing chill emanating from the dogma of predestination. Romanists, Lutherans, Arminians and Libertines have ever charged against Calvinism that its absolute doctrine of predestination, culminating in the perseverance of saints, must necessarily result in a too easy conscience and a dangerous laxity of morals. But Calvinism answers this charge, not by opposing reasoning against reasoning, but by putting a fact of world-wide reputation over against this false deduction of fictitious consequences. It simply asks:— "What rival moral fruits have other religions to oppose if we point to the high moral earnestness of the Puritans?" "Shall we continue in sin that grace may abound" is the old diabolical whisper which the evil spirit hurled against the Holy Apostle himself in the childhood of the Christian Church. And when, in the sixteenth century the Heidelburg Catechism had to defend Calvinism against the shameful charge:—"Does not this doctrine lead to careless and ungodly lives?". Ursinus and Olevianus had to deal with nothing less than the echoing and monotonous repetition of the same old slander. Certainly the ungodly lust to persist in, and even to foster, indwelling sin, yea even Antinomianism itself, again and again abused the Calvinistic confession, seizing it like a shield, to hide the carnal appetites of the unconverted heart. But as little as the mechanical repetition of a written confession had ever anything in common with genuine religion, just so little may the Calvinistic Confession be made responsible for those reverberating

stone pillars, echoing Calvin's formulæ, but without a
grain of Calvinistic earnestness in their heart. He only
is the real Calvinist, and may raise the Calvinistic
banner, who in his own soul, personally, has been
struck by the Majesty of the Almighty, and yielding to
the overpowering might of his eternal Love, has dared
to proclaim this majestic love, over against Satan, and
the world, and the worldliness of his own heart, in the
personal conviction of being chosen by God Himself,
and therefore of having to thank Him and Him alone,
for every grace everlasting. Such an one could not but
tremble before the might and the majesty of God, as a
matter of course accepting His Word as the ruling
principle of His conduct in life;—a principle which has
led so far that for its strong attachment to the Scriptures,
Calvinism has been censured, as being a *nomistic* religion,
but without any warrant. *Nomistic* is the appropriate
name for a religion which proclaims *salvation* to be
attained by the fulfilment of the law, while Calvinism,
on the other hand, in a thoroughly soteriological sense,
never derived salvation but from Christ and the atoning
fruit of His merits.

But it remained the special trait of Calvinism that it
placed the believer *before the face of God*, not only in
His church, but also in his personal, family, social, and
political life. The majesty of God, and the authority
of God press upon the Calvinist in the whole of his
human existence. He is a pilgrim, not in the sense that
he is marching through a world with which he has no
concern, but in the sense that at every step of the long
way he must remember his responsibility to that God

so full of majesty, Who awaits him at his journey's
end. In front of the Portal which opens for him, on the
entrance into Eternity, stands the *Last Judgment*; and
that judgment shall be one broad and comprehensive
test, to ascertain whether the long pilgrimage has been
accomplished with a heart that aimed at God's glory, and
in accordance with the ordinances of the Most High.

What now does the Calvinist mean by his faith in
the ordinances of God? Nothing less than the firmly
rooted conviction that all life has first been in the *thoughts*
of God, before it came to be realized in *Creation*. Hence
all created life necessarily bears in itself a law for its
existence, instituted by God Himself. There is no life
outside us in Nature, without such divine ordinances,—
ordinances which are called the laws of Nature;—a
term which we are willing to accept, provided we understand thereby, not laws orginating *from* Nature, but
laws imposed *upon* Nature. So, there are ordinances
of God for the firmament above, and ordinances for the
earth below, by means of which this world is maintained,
and, as the Psalmist says, These ordinances are the
servants of God. Consequently there are ordinances
of God for our bodies, for the blood that courses
through our arteries, and veins, and for our lungs as the
organs of respiration. And even so are there ordinances
of God, in Logic, to regulate our thoughts; ordinances
of God for our imagination, in the domain of aesthetics; and so, also, strict ordinances of God for the whole
óf human life in the *domain of morals*. Not moral
ordinances in the sense of summary general laws, which
leave the decision in concrete and detailed instances to

ourselves, but just as the ordinance of God determines
the course of the smallest asteroid, as well as the orbit
of the mightiest star, so also these moral ordinances of
God descend to the smallest and most particular details,
stating to us what in every case is to be considered as
the will of God. And those ordinances of God, ruling
both the mightiest problems and the smallest trifles, are
urged upon us, not like the statutes of a law-book, not
like rules which may be read from paper, not like a
codification of life, which could even for a single moment,
exercise any authority of itself,—but they are urged
upon us as the constant will of the Omnipresent and
Almighty God, Who at every instant is determining the
course of life, ordaining its laws, and continually binding
us by His divine authority. The Calvinist does not,
like Kant, ascend in his reasoning from the "*Du Sollst*"
(Thou shalt) to the idea of a lawgiver, but, because
he stands before the face of God, because he sees God,
and walks with God, and feels God in the whole of his
being and existence, therefore he cannot withdraw his
ear from that never silenced "*Thou shalt*", which proceeds continually from his God, in nature, in his body,
in his reason, and in his action.

Thence it follows that the true Calvinist adjusts himself
to these ordinances not by force, as though they were
a yoke of which he would like to rid himself, but
with the same readiness with which we follow a guide
through the desert, recognizing that *we* are ignorant of
the path, which the guide knows, and therefore acknowledging that there is no safety but in closely following
in his footsteps. When our respiration is disturbed, we

try irresistibly and immediately to remove the disturbance, and to make it normal again, *i.e.*, to restore it,
by bringing it again into accordance with the ordinances which God has given for man's respiration. To
suceed in this gives us a feeling of unspeakable relief.
Just so, in every disturbance of the moral life the believer
has to strive as speedily as possible to restore his
spiritual respiration, according to the moral commands
of his God, because only after this restoration can the
inward life again thrive freely in his soul, and renewed
energetic action become possible. Therefore every distinction between general moral ordinances, and more
special *christian* commandments is unknown to him.
Can we imagine that at one time God willed to rule
things in a certain moral order, but that now, in Christ,
He wills to rule it otherwise? As though He were
not the Eternal, the Unchangeable, Who, from the very
hour of creation even unto all eternity had willed, wills,
and shall will and maintain one and the same firm
moral world-order! Verily Christ has swept away the
dust with wich man's sinful limitations had covered up
this world-order, and has made it glitter again in its
original brilliancy. Verily Christ and He alone has
disclosed to us the eternal love of God, which was,
from the beginning, the moving principle of this world-
order. Above all, Christ has strengthened in us the
ability to walk in this world-order with a firm, unfaltering
step. But the world-order itself remains just what it
was from the beginning. It lays full claim, not only to
the believer (as though less were required from the un-
believer), but to every human being and to all human

relationships. Hence Calvinism does not lead us to philo-
sophize on a so-called moral life, as though *we* had to
create, to discover, or to regulate this life. Calvinism
simply places us under the impress of the majesty of
God, and subjects us to His eternal ordinances and
unchangeable commandments. Hence it is that, for the
Calvinist, all ethical study is based on the Law of Sinai,
not as though at that time the moral world-order
began to be fixed, but to honour the Law of Sinai,
as the divinely authentic summary of that original moral
law which God wrote in the heart of man, at his
creation, and which God is re-writing on the tables of
every heart at its conversion. The Calvinist is led to
submit himself to the conscience, not as to an individual
lawgiver, which every person carries about in himself,
but as to a direct *sensus divinitatis*, through which God
Himself stirs up the inner man, and subjects him to His
judgment. He does not hold to religion, with its *dogmatics*,
as a *separate entity*, and then place his moral life with
its ethics as a *second entity* alongside of religion, but
he holds to religion, as placing him in the presence of
God Himself, Who thereby embues him with His divine
will. Love and adoration are, to Calvin, themselves
the motives of every spiritual activity, and thus the
fear of God is imparted to the whole of life as a reality,—
into the family, and into society, into science and art,
into personal life, and into the political career. A redeemed man who in *all* things and in *all* the choices of
life is controlled solely by the most searching, and
heart-stirring reverence for a God Who is ever present
to his consciousness, and Who ever holds him in His

eye;—thus does the Calvinistic type present itself in history. Always and in all things the deepest, the most sacred reverence for the ever-present God as the rule of life,—this is the only true picture of the original Puritan.

The avoidance of the world has never been the Calvinistic mark, but the shibboleth of the Anabaptist. The specific, anabaptistical dogma of "avoidance" proves this. According to this dogma, the Anabaptists, announcing themselves as "saints", were severed from the world. They stood in opposition to it. They refused to take the oath; they abhorred all military service; they condemned the holding of public offices. Here already, they shaped a new world, in the midst of this world of sin, which however had nothing to do with this our present existence. They rejected all obligation and reponsibility towards the old world, and they avoided it systematically, for fear of contamination, and contagion. But this is just what the Calvinist always disputed and denied. It is not true that there are two worlds, a bad one and a good, which are fitted into each other. It is one and the same person whom God created perfect and who afterwards fell, and became a sinner;—and it is this same "ego" of the old sinner who is born again, and who enters into eternal life. So, also, it is one and the same world which once exhibited all the glory of Paradise, which was afterwards smitten with the curse, and which, since the Fall, is upheld by common grace; which has now been redeemed and saved by Christ, in its centre, and which shall pass through the horror of the judgment into the state of glory. For this very reason the Calvinist cannot shut himself up in his church and abandon the world to its fate. He feels, rather, his high calling to push the development of this world to an even higher stage, and to do this in constant accordance with God's ordinance, for the sake of God, upholding, in the midst of so much painful corruption, everything that is honourable, lovely, and of good report among men. Therefore it is that we see in History (if I may be permitted to speak of my own ancestors), that scarcely had Calvinism been firmly established in the Netherlands for a quarter of a century, when there was a rustling of life in all directions, and an indomitable energy was fermenting in every department of human activity, and their commerce and trade, their handicrafts and industry, their agriculture and horticulture, their art and science, flourished with a brilliancy previously unknown, and imparted a new impulse for an entirely new development of life, to the whole of Western Europe.

This admits of only one exception, and this exception I wish both to maintain and to place in its proper light. What I mean is this. Not *every* intimate intercourse with the unconverted world is deemed lawful, by Calvinism, for it placed a barrier against the too unhallowed influence of this world by putting a distinct "veto" upon three things, *card playing, theatres,* and *dancing;*— three forms of amusement which I shall first treat separately, and then set forth in their combined significance.

Card-playing has been placed under a ban by Calvinism,

not as though games of all kinds were forbidden, nor as
though something demoniacal lurked in the cards themselves, but because it fosters in our heart the dangerous
tendency to look away from God, and to put our trust
in *Fortune* or *Luck.* A game which is decided by
keenness of vision, quickness of action, and range of
experience, is ennobling in its character, but a game like
cards, which is chiefly decided by the way in which
the cards are arranged in the pack, and blindly distributed, induces us to attach a certain significance to that
fatal imaginative power, outside of God, called *Chance*
or *Fortune.* To this kind of unbelief, every one of us
is inclined. The fever of stock-gambling shews daily
how much more strongly people are attracted and
influenced by the nod of Fortune, than by solid application to their work. Therefore the Calvinist judged
that the rising generation ought to be guarded against
this dangerous tendency, because, by means of card-
playing it would be fostered. And since the sensation
of God's ever-enduring presence was felt by Calvin
and his adherents as the never-failing source from which
they drew their stern seriousness of life, they could not
help loathing a game which poisoned this source by
placing Fortune above the disposition of God, and the
hankering after chance above the firm confidence in
His will. To fear God, and to bid for the favours of
Fortune, seemed to him as irreconcilable as fire and
water.

Entirely different objections were entertained against
Theatre-going. In itself there is nothing sinful in fiction;
—the power of the imagination is a precious gift of

God Himself. Neither is there any special evil in *dramatic* imagination. How highly did Milton appreciate Shakespeare's Drama, and did not he himself write in dramatic form? Nor did the evil lie in public theatrical representations, as such. Public performances were given for all the people at Geneva, in the Market Place, in Calvin's time, and with his approval. No, that which offended our ancestors was not the comedy or tragedy, nor should have been the opera, in itself, but the *moral sacrifice* which as a rule was demanded of actors and actresses, for the amusement of the public. A theatrical troop, in those days especially, stood, morally, rather low. This low moral standard resulted partly from the fact that the constant and ever-changing presentation of the character of another person, finally hampers the moulding of your personal character; and partly because our modern Theatres, unlike the Greek, have introduced the presence of women on the stage, the prosperity of the Theatre being too often gauged by the measure in which a woman jeopardizes the most sacred treasures God entrusts to her, her stainless name, and irreproachable conduct. Certainly, a strictly moral Theatre is very well conceivable; but with the exception of a few large cities, such Theatres would neither be sufficiently patronized nor could exist financially; and the actual fact remains that, taking all the world over, the prosperity of a Theatre often increases in proportion to the moral degradation of the actors. Too often therefore—Hall Caine in his "*Christian*" corroborated once more the sad truth — the prosperity of Theatres is purchased at the cost of manly character, and of female purity. And the purchase of delight for the ear and the eye at the price of such a moral hecatomb, the Calvinist, who honoured whatever was human in man for the sake of God, could not but condemn.

Finally, so far as the *dance* is concerned, even worldly papers, like the Parisian "*Figaro*", at present justify the position of the Calvinist. Only recently an article in this paper called attention to the moral pain with which a father takes his daughter into the Ball-room for the first time. This moral pain, it declared, is evident, in Paris at least, to all who are familiar with the whisperings, indecent looks and actions prevalent in those pleasure-loving circles. Here, also, the Calvinist does not protest against the Dance itself, but exclusively, against the impurity to which it is often in danger of leading.

With this I return to the barrier of which I spoke. Our fathers perceived excellently well that it was just these three: Dancing, Card-playing, and Theatre-going, with which the world was madly in love. In worldly circles these pleasures were not regarded as secondary trifles, but honoured as all-important matters: and whoever dared to attack them, exposed himself to the bitterest scorn and enmity. For this very reason, they recognized, in these three, the *Rubicon* which no true Calvinist could cross without sacrificing his earnestness to dangerous mirth, and the fear of the Lord to often far from spotless pleasures. And now may I ask, has not the result justified their strong and brave protest? Even yet, after a lapse of three centuries, you will find, in my Calvinistic country, in Scotland, and in your own States, entire social circles into which this worldliness

is never allowed to enter, but in which the richness of
human life has turned, from without, inward, and in
which, as the result of a sound spiritual concentration,
there has been developed such a deep sense of everything
high, and such an energy for everything holy, as to
excite the envy even of our antagonists. Not only has
the wing of the butterfly in those circles been preserved
intact, but even the golddust upon this wing shines as
brilliantly as ever.

This now is the proof to which I invite your respectful
attention. Our age is far ahead of the Calvinistic age
in its overflowing mass of ethical essays and treatises
and learned expositions. Philosophers and Theologians
really vie with one another in discovering for us (or in
hiding from us, just as you may be pleased to put it)
the straight road in the domain of morals. But there
is something that all this host of learned scholars have
not been able to do. They have not been able to restore
moral firmness to the enfeebled public conscience.

Rather must we complain that ever more and more
the foundations of our moral building are gradually
being loosened and unsettled, until finally there remains
not one stronghold left of which the people in their
wider ranks can feel that it guarantees *moral certainty*
for the Future. Statesmen and Jurists are openly proclaiming the right of the strongest; the ownership of
property is called stealing; free love has been advocated;
and honesty is ridiculed. A pantheist has dared to put
Jesus and Nero on the same footing; and Nietzsche,
going further still, deemed Christ's blessing of the meek
to be the curse of humanity.

Now compare with all this the marvellous results of three centuries of Calvinism. Calvinism understood that the world was not to be saved by ethical philosophizing, but only by the restoration of tenderness of conscience. Therefore it did not indulge in reasoning, but appealed directly to the soul, and placed it face to face with the Living God, so that the heart trembled, at His holy majesty, and in that majesty, discovered the glory of His love. And when, going back in this historical review, you observe how thoroughly corrupt and rotten Calvinism found the world, to what depth moral life at that time had sunk, in the courts, and among the people, in the clergy, and among the leaders of science, among men and women, among the higher and the lower classes of society:—then what censor among you will dare to deny the palm of moral victory to Calvinism, which in one generation, though hunted from the battlefield to the scaffold, created, throughout five nations at once, wide serious groups of noble men, and still nobler women, hitherto unsurpassed in the loftiness of their ideal conceptions and unequalled in the power of their moral self-control.

THIRD LECTURE.

My third lecture leaves the sanctuary of religion and enters upon the domain of the State—the first transition from the sacred circle to the secular field of human life. Only now therefore we proceed, summarily and in principle, to combat the unhistorical suggestion, that Calvinism represents an exclusively ecclesiastical and dogmatic movement.

The religious momentum of Calvinism has placed, also beneath political Society, a fundamental conception, all its own, just because it not merely pruned the branches and clean the stem, but reached down to the very root of our human life.

That this *had to be so* becomes evident at once to everyone who is able to appreciate the fact that no political scheme has ever become dominant, which was not founded in a specific religious or antireligious conception. And that this *has* been the fact, as regards Calvinism, may appear from the political changes which it has effected in those three historic lands of political freedom, the Netherlands, England and America.

Every competent historian will without exception confirm the words of Bancroft:—"The fanatic for Calvinism was a fanatic for liberty, for in the moral warfare for freedom, his creed was a part of his army, and his most faithful ally in the battle." 1)) And Groen van Prinsterer has thus expressed it: "In Calvinism lies the origin and guarantee of our constitutional liberties." That Calvinism has led public law into new paths, first in Western Europe, then in two Continents, and to-day more and more among all civilized nations, is admitted by all scientific students, if not yet fully by public opinion.

But for the purpose I have in view, the mere statement of this important fact is insufficient.

In order that the influence of Calvinism on our political development may be felt, it must be shown, for what fundamental political conceptions Calvinism has opened the door, and how these political conceptions sprang from its root principle.

This dominating principle was not, soteriologically, justification by faith, but, in the widest sense cosmologically, *the Sovereignty of the Triune God over the whole Cosmos*, in all its spheres and kingdoms, visible and invisible. A *primordial* Sovereignty which eradiates in mankind in a threefold deduced supremacy, *viz.*, 1. The Sovereignty in the *State;* 2. The Sovereignty in *Society;* and 3. The Sovereignty in the *Church.*

Allow me to argue this matter in detail by pointing out to you how this threefold deduced Sovereignty was understood by Calvinism.

1) BANCROFT, *History of the United States of America.* Fifteenth Ed. Boston 1853, I. 464. Ed. New York, 1891, I. 319.

First then a deduced Sovereignty in that political sphere, which is defined as *the State*. And then we admit that the impulse to form states arises from man's social nature, which was expressed already by Aristotle, when he called man a "ζῷον πολιτικόν." God might have created men as disconnected individuals, standing side by side and without genealogical coherence. Just as Adam was separately created, the second and third and every further man might have been individually called into existence; but this was *not* the case.

Man is created from man, and by virtue* of his birth he is organically united with the whole race. Together we form *one humanity*, not only with those who are living now, but also with all the generations behind us and with all those who shall come after us,—pulverized into millions though we may be. All the human race is from *one blood*. The conception of *States*, however, which subdivide the earth into continents, and each continent into morsels, does not harmonize with this idea. Then only would the organic unity of our race be realized politically, if *one State* could embrace all the world, and if the whole of humanity were associated in one world-empire. Had sin not intervened, no doubt, this would actually have been so. If sin, as a disintegrating force, had not divided humanity into different sections, nothing would have marred or broken the organic unity of our race. And the mistake of the Alexanders, and of the Augusti, and of the Napoleons was not, that they were charmed with the thought of the *One World-empire*, but it was this—that they endeavoured to realize this idea notwithstanding that the force of sin had dissolved our unity.

In like manner the international cosmopolitan endeavours of the Social-democracy present, in their conception of union, an ideal, which on this very account charms
us, even when we are aware that they try to reach the
unattainable, in endeavouring to realize this high and
holy ideal, now and in a sinful world. Nay even Anarchy,
conceived as the attempt to undo all mechanical connections among men, together with the undoing of all
human authority, and to encourage, in their stead, the
growth of a new organic tie, arising from nature itself,—
I say, all this is nothing but a looking backward after
a lost paradise.

For indeed without sin there would have been neither
magistrate nor state-order; but political life, in its entirety,
would have evolved itself, after a patriarchal fashion,
from the life of the family. Neither bar of justice, nor
police nor army, nor navy is conceivable in a world
without sin; and thus every rule and ordinance and law
would drop away, even as all control and assertion of
the power of the magistrate would disappear, were life
to develop itself, normally and without hindrance, from
its own organic impulse. Who binds up, where nothing
is broken? Who uses crutches, where the limbs are sound?

Every State-formation, every assertion of the power
of the magistrate, every mechanical means of compelling
order and of guaranteeing a safe course of life is therefore
always something unnatural; something, against which the
deeper aspirations of our nature rebel; and which, on this
·very account, may become the source both of a dreadful
abuse of power, on the part of those who exercise it, and of
a contumacious revolt on the part the multitude.   Thus

originated the battle of the ages between *Authority* and *Liberty*, and in this battle it was the very innate thirst for liberty, which proved itself the God-ordained means to bridle the authority, wheresoever it degenerated into despotism. And thus all true conception of the nature of the State and of the assumption of authority by the magistrate, and on the other hand all true conception of the right and duty of the people to defend liberty, depend on what Calvinism has here placed in the foreground, as the primordial truth,— *that God has instituted the magistrates, by reason of sin.*

In this one thought are hidden both the *light-side* and the *shady-side* of the life of the State. The *shady-side*, for this multitude of states ought not to exist; there should be only one world-empire. These magistrates rule mechanically and do not harmonize with our nature. And this authority of government is exercised by sinful *men*, and is therefore subject to all manner of despotic ambitions. But the *light-side* also, for a sinful humanity, without division in states, without law and government, and without ruling authority, would be a veritable hell on earth; or at least a repetition of that which existed on earth, when God drowned the first degenerate race, in the deluge. Calvinism has therefore, by its deep conception of sin, laid bare the true root of state-life, and has taught us two things: First—that we have gratefully to receive, from the hand of God, the institution of the State with its magistrates, as a means of preservation, now indeed indispensable. And on the other hand also that, by virtue of our natural impulse, we must ever watch against the danger, which lurks, for our personal liberty, in the power of the State.

But Calvinism has done more. In Politics also it taught us, that the *human* element—here *the people*—may not be considered as the principal thing, so that God is only dragged in to help this people in the hour of its need; but on the contrary that God, in His Majesty, must. flame before the eyes of every nation, and that all nations together are to be reckoned before Him as a drop of a bucket and as the small dust of the balances. From the ends of the earth God cites all nations and peoples before His high judgment seat. For God created the nations. They exist for Him. They are His own. And therefore all these nations, and in them all humanity, must exist for His glory and consequently after his ordinances, in order that in their well-being, when they walk after His ordinances, His divine wisdom may shine forth.

When therefore humanity falls apart through sin, in a multiplicity of separate peoples; when sin, in the bosom of these nations, separates men and tears them apart, and when sin reveals itself in all manner of shame and unrighteousness,—the glory of God demands that these horrors be bridled, that order return to this chaos, and that a compulsory force, from without, assert itself to make human society a possibility.

This right is possessed by God, and by Him alone,

No man has the right to rule over another man, otherwise such a right necessarily, and immediately becomes, the *right of the strongest.* As the tiger in the jungle rules over the defenceless antilope, so on

the banks of the Nile a Pharaoh ruled over the progenitors of the fellaheen of Egypt.

Nor can a group of men, by contract, from their own
right, compel you to obey a fellow-man. What binding
force is there for me in the allegation, that ages ago
one of my progenitors made a "Contrat Social", with
other men of that time? As man I stand, free and bold,
over against the most powerful of my fellow-men.

I do not speak of the family, for here organic, natural
ties rule; but in the sphere of the State I do not yield
or bow down to anyone, who is man, as I am.

Authority over men cannot arise from men. Just as
little from a majority over against a minority, for history
shows, almost on every page, that very often the *minority
was right*. And thus to the first Calvinistic thesis that
sin alone has necessitated the institution of governments,
this second and no less momentous thesis is added that:
*all authority of governments on earth, originates from
the Sovereignty of God alone*. When God says to me,
"obey", then I humbly bow my head, without compro-
mising in the least my personal dignity, as a man. For,
in like proportion as you degrade yourself, by bowing
low to a child of man, whose breath is in his nostrils;
so, on the other hand do you raise yourself, if you
submit to the authority of the Lord of heaven and earth.

Thus the word of Scripture stands: "By Me kings
reign", or as the apostle has elsewhere declared: "The
powers, that be, are ordained of God. Therefore he that
resisteth the power, withstandeth the ordinance of God".
The magistrate is an instrument of "common grace", to
thwart all license and outrage and to shield the good

against the evil. But he is more. Besides all this he is instituted by God as *His Servant*, in order that he may preserve the glorious work of God, in the creation of humanity, from total destruction. Sin attacks God's handiwork, God's plan, God's justice, God's honour, as the supreme Artificer and Builder. Thus God, ordaining the powers that be, in order that, through their instrumentality, He might maintain *His* justice against the strivings of sin, has given to the magistrate the terrible right of life and death. Therefore all the powers that be, whether in empires or in republics, in cities or in states, rule *"by the grace of God."* For the same reason justice bears a holy character. And from the same motive every citizen is bound to obey, not only from dread of punishment, but for the sake of conscience.

Further Calvin has expressly stated that authority, as such, is in no way affected by the question, how a government is instituted and in what form it reveals itself. It is well known that personally he preferred *a republic*, and that he cherished no predilection for a monarchy, as if this were the divine and ideal form of government. This indeed would have been the case in a sinless state. For had sin not entered, God would have remained the sole king of all men, and this condition will return, in the glory to come, when God once more will be all and in all. God's own direct government is absolutely *monarchical*; no monotheist will deny it. But Calvin considered a co-operation of many persons under mutual control, *i.e.*, a *republic*, desirable, now that a mechanical institution of government is necessitated by reason of sin.

In his system however, this could only amount to
a gradual difference in practical excellency, but never
to a fundamental difference, as regards the essence of
authority. He considers a monarchy and an aristocracy,
as well as a democracy, both possible and practicable
forms of government; provided it be unchangeably
maintained, that no one on earth can claim authority
over his fellow-men, unless it be laid upon him "*by the.
grace of God*"; and therefore, the ultimate duty of
obedience, is imposed upon us not by man, but by
God Himself.

The question how those persons, who by divine
authority are to be clothed with power, are indicated,
cannot, according to Calvin, be answered alike for all
peoples and for all time. And yet he does not hesitate
to state, in an ideal sense, that the most desirable
conditions exists, *where the people itself chooses its
own magistrates*. Where such a condition exists he
thinks that the people should gratefully recognize
therein a favour of God, precisely as it has been
expressed in the preamble of more than one of your
constitutions;—"Grateful to almighty God that He gave
us the power to choose our own magistrates." In his
Commentary on Samuel, Calvin therefore admonishes
such peoples:—"And ye, O peoples, to whom God gave
the liberty to choose your own magistrates, see to it,
that ye do not forfeit this favour, by electing to the
positions of highest honour, rascals and enemies of God."

I may add that the popular choice gains the day,
as a matter of course, where no other rule exists, or
where the existing rule falls away. Wherever new States

have been founded, except by conquest or force, the
first government has always been founded by popular
choice; and so also where the highest authority had fallen
into disorder, either by want of a determination of the
right of succession, or through the violence of revolution, it has always been the people who through their
representatives, claimed the right to restore it. But with
equal decision, Calvin asserts that God has the sovereign
power, in the way of His dispensing providence, to
take from a people this most desirable condition, or
never to bestow it at all, when a nation is unfit for it,
or, by its sin, has utterly forfeited the blessing.

The historic development of a people shows, as a
matter of course, in what other ways authority is
bestowed. This bestowal may flow from the right of
inheritance, as in a hereditary monarchy. It may result
from a hard-fought war, even as Pilate had power over
Jesus, "given him from above." It may proceed from
electors, as it did in the old German empire. It may
rest with the States of the country, as was the case
in the old Dutch republic. In a word it may assume a
variety of forms, because there is an endless difference
in the development of nations. A form of government
like your own, could not exist one day in China. Even
now, the people of Russia are unfit for any form of
constitutional government. And among the Kaffirs and
Hottentots of Africa, even a government, such as exists
in Russia, would be wholly inconceivable. All this is
determined and appointed by God, through the hidden
counsel of His providence.   .

All this, however, is no *theocracy*. A theocracy was

only found in Israel, because in Israel, God intervened
immediately. For both by *Urim and Thummim* and
by *Prophecy;* both by His saving miracles, and by His
chastising judgments, He held in His own hand the
jurisdiction and the leadership of His people. But the
Calvinistic confession of the sovereignty of God, holds
good for *all* the world, is true for all nations, and is
of force in all authority, which man exercises over man;
even in the authority which parents possess over their
children. It is therefore a political faith which may be
summarily expressed in these three theses:— 1. God
only—and never any creature—is possessed of sovereign
rights, in the destiny of the nations, because God alone
created them, maintains them by His Almighty power,
and rules them, by His ordinances. 2. Sin has, in the
realm of politics, broken down the direct government of
God, and therefore the exercise of authority, for the
purpose of government, has subsequently been invested
in men, as a mechanical remedy. And 3. In whatever
form this authority may reveal itself, man never possesses
power over his fellow-man, in any other way than by
an authority which descends upon him from the majesty
of God.

———————

Directly opposed to this Calvinistic confession there
are two other theories. That of the *Popular-sovereignty*,
as it has been anti-theistically proclaimed at Paris in
1789; and that of *State-sovereignty*, as it has of late
been developed by the historico-pantheistic school of
Germany. Both these theories are at heart identical,

but for the sake of clearness they demand a separate treatment.

What was it, that impelled and animated the spirits of men in the great French revolution? Indignation at abuses, which had crept in? A horror of a crowned despotism? A noble defense of the rights and liberties of the people? In part certainly, but in all this there is so little that is sinful, that even a Calvinist gratefully recognizes, in these three particulars, the divine judgment, which at that time was executed at Paris.

But the impelling force of the French Revolution did not lie in this hatred of abuses. When Edmund Burke compares the "glorious Revolution" of 1688, with the principle of the Revolution of 1789, he says—: "Our revolution and that of France are just the reverse of each other, in almost every particular, and in the whole spirit of the transaction." 1)

This same Edmund Burke, was so bitter an antagonist the French revolution, has manfully defended your own rebellion against England, as "arising from a principle of energy, showing itself in this good people the main cause of a free spirit, the most adverse to all implicit submission of mind and opinion."

The three great revolutions in the Calvinistic world left untouched the glory of God, nay they even proceeded from the acknowledgment of His majesty. Every one will admit this of our rebellion against Spain, under William the Silent. Nor has it even been doubted of the "glorious Revolution", which was crowned by the

1) BURKE, *Works* III p. 25 Ed. McLean, London.

arrival of William III, of Orange, and the overthrow of
the Stuarts. But it is equally true of your own Revolution. It is expressed, in so many words, in the
Declaration of independence, by John Hancock, that
the Americans asserted themselves by virtue—"of the
law of nature and of nature's God"; that they acted—
"as endowed by the Creator with certain unalienable
rights"; that they appealed to—"the Supreme Judge of
the world for the rectitude of their intention"; 1. and
that they sent forth their "declaration of Independence"—
"with a firm reliance on the protection of Divine Providence". 2. In the "Articles of Confederation" it is
confessed in the preamble,—"that it hath pleased the
great Governor of the world to incline the hearts of
the legislators." 3. It is also declared in the preamble
of the Constitution of many of the States:—"Grateful to
Almighty God for the civil, political and religious liberty,
which He has so long permitted us to enjoy and looking
unto Him, for a blessing upon our endeavours." 4.
God is there honoured as "the Sovereign Ruler", 5.
and the "Legislator of the Universe" 6. and it is there
specifically admitted, that from God alone the people
received "the right to choose their own form of government." 7. In one of the meetings of the Convention,
Franklin proposed, in a moment of supreme anxiety,
that they should ask wisdom from God in prayer. And

1) *American Constitutions*, by Franklin B. Hugh, Albany Weed Parsons
& Co. 1872. Vol. I. p. 5.
2) Ibidem p. 8.   3) p. 19.
4) Ibidem II, p. 549.
5) Ibidem p. 555.   6) p. 555.   7) p. 549.

if any one should still doubt whether or not, the American revolution was homogeneous with that of Paris, this doubt is fully set at rest, by the bitter fight, in 1793, between Jefferson and Hamilton. Therefore it remains, as the German historian Von Holtz stated it: "Es wäre Thorheit zu sagen dass die Rousseauschen Schriften einen Einfluss auf die Entwicklung in America ausgeübt haben." 1) ("Mere madness would it be to say that the American revolution borrowed its impelling energy from Rousseau and his writings.") Or as Hamilton himself expressed it, that he considered "the French Revolution to be no more akin to the American Revolution, than the faithless wife in a French novel is like the Puritan matron in New-England." 2)

The French Revolution is in principle distinct from all these *national* revolutions, which were undertaken with praying lips and with trust in the help of God. The French Revolution ignores God. It opposes God. It

---

1) Von Holtz, *Verfassung und Democratie der Vereinigten Staten von America.* Dusseldorf. 1873 I p. 96.

2) John F. Morse, *Thomas Jefferson,* Boston 1883, p. 147. In a positively *Christian* sense Hamilton proposed in a letter to Bayard (April 1801) the founding of "A Christian Constitutional Society", and wrote in another letter, quoted by Henry Cabot Lodge, *Alexander Hamilton,* Boston 1892, p. 256: "When I find the doctrines of Atheism openly advanced in the Parisian Convention, and heard with loud applause; when I see the sword of fanaticism extended to force a political creed upon citizens, who were invited to submit to the arms of France as the harbingers of Liberty; when I behold the hand of rapacity outstretched to prostrate and ravish the monuments of religious worship, I acknowledge, that I am glad to believe, *that there is no real resemblance between what was the cause of America and the cause of France*".

refuses to recognize a deeper ground of political life than that which is found in nature, that is, in this instance, in man himself. Here the first article of the confession of the most absolute infidelity is—"ni Dieu ni maître". The sovereign God is dethroned and man with his free will is placed on the vacant seat. It is the will of man which determines all things. All power, all authority proceeds from man. Thus one comes from the individual man to the many men; and in those many men conceived as *the people*, there is thus hidden the deepest fountain of all sovereignty. There is no question, as in your Constitution, of a sovereignty derived from God, which He, under certain conditions, implants in the people. Here an original sovereignty asserts itself, which everywhere and in all states can only proceed from the people itself, having no deeper root than in the human will. It is a sovereignty of the people therefore, which is perfectly identical with atheism. And herein lies its self-abasement. In the sphere of Calvinism, as also in your *Declaration*, the knee is bowed to God, while over against man the head is proudly lifted up. But here, from the standpoint of the sovereignty of the people, the fist is defiantly clenched against God, while man grovels before his fellow-men, tinseling over this self-abasement by the ludicrous fiction that, thousands of years ago, men, of whom no one has any remembrance, concluded a political contract, or, as they called it, *"Contrat Social"*. Now, do you ask for the result? Then, let History tell you how the rebellion of the Netherlands, the "glorious Revolution" of England and your own rebellion against the British Crown have brought liberty to honour; and

answer for yourself the question : Has the French Revolution resulted in anything else but the shackling of
liberty in the irons of State-omnipotence? Indeed no
country in our 19th century, has had a sadder State-
history than France.

No wonder that scientific Germany has broken away
from this fictitious sovereignty of the people, since the
days of De Savigny and Niebuhr. The Historical school,
founded by these eminent men, has pilloried the a-prioristic
fiction of 1789. Every historical connoisseur now ridicules
it. Only that which they recommended instead of it,
bears no better stamp.

Now it was to be not the sovereignty of the people,
but the *Sovereignty of the State*, a product of Germanic
philosophical pantheism. Ideas are incarnated in the
reality, and among these the idea of the State was the
highest, the richest, the most perfect idea of the relation
between man and man. Thus the State became a mystical
conception. The State was considered as a mysterious
being, with a hidden *ego*; with a State-*consciousness*,
slowly developing; and with an increasing potent State-
will, which by a slow process endeavoured to blindly
reach the highest State-*aim*. The people was not understood as with Rousseau, to be the sum total of the
individuals. It was correctly seen that a people is no
aggregate, but an organic whole. This organism must
of necessity have its organic members. Slowly these
organs arrived at their historic development. By these
organs, the will of the State operates, and everything
must bow before this will. This sovereign State-will
might reveal itself in a republic, in a monarchy, in a

8

Caesar, in an Asiatic despot, in a tyrant as Philip of Spain, or in a dictator like Napoleon. All these were but forms, in which the one State-idea incorporated itself; the stages of development in a never ending process. But in whatever form this mystical being of the State revealed itself, the idea remained supreme: the State shortly asserted its sovereignty and for every member of the State, it remained the touchstone of wisdom to . give way to this State-apotheosis.

Thus all transcendent right in God, to which the oppressed lifted up his face, falls away. There is no other right, but the immanent right which is written down in the law. The law is right, not because its contents are in harmony with the eternal principles of right, but because *it is law*. If on the morrow it fixes the very opposite, this also must be right. And the fruit of this deadening theory is, as a matter of course, that the consciousness of right is blunted, that all fixedness of right departs from our minds, and that all higher enthusiasm for right is extinguished. That which exists is good, because it exists; and it is no longer the will of God, of Him Who created us and knows us, but it becomes the ever-changing will of the State, which, having no one above itself, actually becomes *God*, and has to decide how our life and our existence shall be.

And when you further consider that this mystical State expresses and enforces its will only through men—what further proof is demanded that this state-sovereignty, even as popular sovereignty, does not outgrow the abasing subjection of man to his fellow-man and never ascends to a duty of submission which finds its cogency in the conscience?

Therefore in opposition both to the atheistic popular-sovereignty of the Encyclopedians, and the pantheistic state-sovereignty of German philosophers, the Calvinist maintains the sovereignty of God, as the source of all authority among men.   The Calvinist upholds the highest and best in our aspirations, by placing every man and every people before the face of our Father in heaven. He takes cognizance of the fact of sin, which erstwhile was juggled away in 1789, and which now, in pessimistic extravagance, in accounted the essence of our being. Calvinism points to the difference between the natural concatnation of our organic society and the mechanical tie, which the authority of the magistrate imposes. It makes it easy for us to obey authority, because, in all authority, it causes us to honour the demand of divine sovereignty.   It lifts us from an obedience born of dread of the strong arm, into an obedience for conscience sake. It teaches us to look upward from the existing law to the source of the eternal Right in God, and it creates in us the indomitable courage incessantly to protest against the unrighteousness of the law in the name of this highest Right.   And, however, powerfully the State may assert itself and oppress the free individual development, above that powerful State there is always glittering, before our soul's eye, as infinitely more powerful, the majesty of the King of kings; Whose righteous bar ever maintains the right of appeal for all the oppressed, and unto Whom the prayer of the people ever ascends, to bless our nation and, in that nation, us and our house!

So much for the sovereignty of the State. We now come to *sovereignty in the sphere of Society.*

In a Calvinistic sense we understand hereby, that the family, the business, science, art and so forth are all social spheres, which do not owe their existence to the State, and which do not derive the law of their life from the superiority of the state, but obey a high authority within their own bosom; an authority which rules, by the grace of God, just as the sovereignty of the State does.

This involves the antithesis between *State* and *Society*, but upon this condition, that we do not conceive this society as a conglomerate, but as analysed in its organic parts, to honour, in each of these parts, the independent character, which appertains to them.

In this independent character a special *higher authority* is of necessity involved and this highest authority we intentionally call—*sovereignty in the individual social spheres,* in order that it may be sharply and decidedly expressed that these different developments of social life have *nothing above themselves but God*, and that the State cannot intrude here, and has nothing to command in their domain. As you feel at once, this is the deeply interesting question of our *civil liberties.* 1)

It is here of the highest importance sharply to keep in mind the difference in grade between the *organic* life of society and the *mechanical* character of the govern-

---

1) Cf. Dr. A. KUIJPER. *Calvinism the source and garantee of our constitutional liberties*, 1873, and Dr. A. KUIJPER, *Sovereignty in the spheres of Society*, 1880.

ment. Whatever among men originates directly from creation, is possessed of all the data for its development, in human nature as such. You see this at once in the family and in the connection of blood relations and other ties. From the duality of man and woman marriage arises. From the original existence of *one* man and *one* woman monogamy comes forth. The children exist by reason of the innate power of reproduction. Naturally the children are connected as brothers and sisters. And when by and by these children, in their turn, marry again, as a matter of course all those connections originate from blood-relationship and other ties, which dominate the whole of family-life. In all this there is nothing mechanical. The development is spontaneous, just as that of the stem and the branches of a plant. True, sin here also has exerted its disturbing influence and has distorted much which was intended for a blessing, into a curse. But this fatal efficiency of sin has been stopped by common grace. Free-love may try to dissolve, and the concubinate to desecrate, the holiest tie, as it pleases; but, for the vast majority of our race marriage remains the foundation of human society and the family retains its position, as the primordial sphere in sociology.

The same may be said of the other spheres of life.

Nature about us may have lost the glory of paradise, by reason of sin, and the earth may bear thorns and thistles, so that we can eat our bread only in the sweat of our brow; notwithstanding all this the chief aim of all human effort remains, what it was by virtue of our creation and before the fall,—namely *dominion over nature*. And this dominion cannot be acquired, except

by the exercise of the powers, which, by virtue of
the ordinances of creation, are innate in nature itself.
Accordingly all Science is only the application to the
cosmos of the powers of investigation and thought,
created within us; and Art is nothing but the natural
productivity of the potencies of our imagination. When
we admit therefore that sin, though arrested by "common grace", has caused many modifications of these
several expressions of life, which originated only after
paradise was lost, and will disappear again, with the
coming of the Kingdom of glory;—we still maintain that
the fundamental character of these expressions remains
as it was originally. All together they form the life of
creation, in accord with the ordinances of creation, and
therefore are *organically* developed.

But the case is wholly different with the assertion of
the powers of government. For though it be admitted
that even without sin the need would have asserted
itself of combining the many families, in a higher unity;
this unity would have *internally* been bound up in the
Kingship of God, which would have ruled regularly,
directly and harmoniously in the hearts of all men,
and which would *externally* have incorporated itself in
a patriarchal hierarchy. Thus no States would have
existed, but only one organic world-empire, with God
as its King; exactly what is prophesied for the future
which awaits us, when all sin shall have disappeared.

But it is exactly this, which sin has now eliminated
from our human life. This unity does no longer exist.
This government of God can no longer assert itself.
This patriarchal hierarchy has been destroyed. A world-

empire neither cannot be established nor ought it to be.
For in this very desire consisted the contumacy of the
building of Babel's tower. Thus peoples and nations originated. These peoples formed States. And over these
States God appointed *governments*. And thus, if I may be
allowed the expression, it is not a natural head, which
organically grew from the body of the people, but a
mechanical head, which from without has been placed
upon the trunk of the nation. A mere remedy therefore, for a wrong condition supervening. A stick placed
beside the plant to hold it up, since without it, by reason
of its inherent weakness, it would fall to the ground.

The principal characteristic of government is the
right of life and death. According to the apostolic
testimony the magistrate bears the sword, and this
sword has a threefold meaning. It is the sword of
justice, to mete out corporeal punishment to the criminal.
Is is the sword of *war* to defend the honour and the
rights and the interests of the State against its enemies.
And it is the sword of *order*, to thwart at home all
forcible rebellion. Luther and his co-Reformers have
correctly pointed out that the institution proper and
the full investiture of the magistrate with power were
only brought about after the flood, when God commanded that capital punishment should fall upon him
who shed man's blood. The right of taking life belongs
only to Him, who can give life, *i.e.*, to God; and therefore no one on earth is invested with this authority,
except it be God-given. On this account, Roman law,
which committed the *jus vitae et necis* to the father and
to the slave-owner, stands intrinsically much lower, than

the law of Moses, which knows no other capital punishment but that by the magistrate and at his command.

The highest duty of the government remains therefore unchangeably that of *justice*, and in the second place it has to care for the people as an unit, partly *at home*, in order that its unity may grow ever deeper and may not be disturbed, and partly *abroad*, lest the national existence suffer harm. The consequence of all this is that on the one hand, in a people, all sorts of *organic* phenomena of life arise, from its *social* spheres, but that, high above all these, the *mechanical* unifying force of the government is observable. From this arises all friction and clashing. For the government is always inclined, with its *mechanical* authority, to invade social life, to subject it and mechanically to arrange it. But on the other hand social life always endeavours to shake off the authority of the government, just as this endeavour at the present time again culminates in social-democracy and in anarchism, both of which aim at nothing less than the total overthrow of the institution of authority. But leaving these two extremes alone, it will be admitted that all healthy life of people or state has ever been the historical consequence of the struggle between these two powers. It was the so called "constitutional government", which endeavoured more firmly to regulate the mutual relation of these two. And in this struggle Calvinism was the first to take its stand. For just in proportion as it honoured the authority of the magistrate, instituted by God, did it lift up that *second sovereignty*, which had been implanted by God in the social spheres, in accordance with the ordinances of creation.

It demanded for both independence in their own sphere and regulation of the relation between both, not by the executive, but *under the law*. And by this stern demand, Calvinism may be said to have generated constitutional public law, from its own fundamental idea.

The testimony of history is unassailable that this constitutional public law has not flourished in Roman Catholic or in Lutheran States, but among the nations of a Calvinistic type. The idea is here fundamental therefore that the sovereignty of God, in its descent upon men, separates itself into two spheres. On the one hand the mechanical sphere of *State-authority*, and on the other hand the organic sphere of the authority of the *Social circles*. And in both these spheres the inherent authority is sovereign, that is to say, it has above itself nothing but God.

Now for the mechanically coercing authority of the government any further explanation is superfluous, not so, however, for the organic social authority.

Nowhere is the dominating character of this organic social authority more plainly discernable than in the sphere of Science. In the introduction to an edition of the "Sententiae" of Lombard and of the "Summa Theologica" of Thomas Aquinas, the learned Thomist wrote: —"The work of Lombard has ruled one hundred and fifty years and has produced Thomas, and after him the 'Summa' of Thomas has ruled all Europe (totam Europam rexit) during five full centuries and has generated all the subsequent Theologians". 1) Suppose we

1) Editon of Migne at Paris 1841. Tome I, proof 1.

admit that this language is overbold, yet the idea, here expressed, is unquestionably correct. The dominion of men like Aristotle and Plato, Lombard and Thomas, Luther and Calvin, Kant and Darwin, extends, for each of them, over a field of ages. Genius is a *sovereign* power ; it forms schools; it lays hold on the spirits of men, with irresistible might; and it exercises an immeasurable influence on the whole condition of human life. This sovereignty of genius is a gift of God, possessed only by His grace. It is subject to no one and is reponsible to Him alone Who has granted it this ascendency.

The same phenomenon is observable in the sphere of Art. Every *maëstro* is a king in the Palace of Art, not by the law of inheritance or by appointment, but only by the grace of God. And these maëstros also impose authority, and are subject to no one, but rule over all and in the end receive from all the homage due to their artistic superiority.

And the same is to be said of the sovereign power of personality. There is no equality of persons. There are weak narrow-minded persons, with no broader expanse of wings than a common sparrow; but there are also broad, imposing characters, with the wing-stroke of the eagle. Among the last you will find a few of royal grandeur, and these rule in their own sphere, whether people draw back from them or thwart them; usually waxing all the stronger, the more they are opposed. And this entire process is carried out in all the spheres of life. In the labour of the mechanic, in the shop, or on the exchange, in commerce, on the sea, in the field of benevolence and philanthropy. Everywhere one man is more powerful than the other, by his personality, by his talent and by circumstances. Dominion is exercised everywhere; but it is a dominion which works organically; not by virtue of a State-investiture, but from life's sovereignty itself.

In relation herewith, and on entirely the same ground of organic superiority, there exists, side by side with this personal sovereignty, the sovereignty of *the sphere*. The University exercises scientific dominion; the Academy of fine arts is possessed of art-power; the guild exercised a technical dominion; the trades-union rules over labour; —and each of these spheres or corporations is conscious of the power of exclusive independent judgment and authoritative action, within its proper sphere of operation. Behind these organic spheres, with intellectual, aesthetical and technical sovereignty, the sphere of the family opens itself, with its right of marriage, domestic peace, education and possession; and in this sphere also the natural head is conscious of exercising an inherent authority,—not because the government allows it, but because God has imposed it. Paternal authority roots itself in the very life-blood and is proclaimed in the fifth Commandment. And so also finally it may be remarked that the social life of cities and villages forms a sphere of existence, which arises from the very necessities of life, and which therefore must be autonomous.

In many different directions we see therefore that sovereignty in one's own sphere asserts itself— 1. In the social sphere, by personal superiority. 2. In the corporative sphere of universities, guilds, associations, etc. 3. In the domestic sphere of the family and of married life, and 4. In communal autonomy.

In all these four spheres the State-government cannot impose its laws, but must reverence the innate law of life. God rules in these spheres, just as supremely and sovereignly through his chosen *virtuosi*, as He exercises dominion in the sphere of the State itself, through his chosen *magistrates.*

Bound by its own mandate therefore the government may neither ignore nor modify nor disrupt the divine mandate, under which these social spheres stand. The sovereignty, by the grace of God, of the government is here set aside and limited, for God's sake, by another sovereignty, which is equally divine in origin. Neither the life of science nor of art, nor of agriculture, nor of industry, nor of commerce, nor of navigation, nor of the family, nor of human relationship may be coerced to suit itself to the grace of the government. The State may never become an octopus, which stifles the whole of life. It must occupy its own place, on its own root, among all the other trees of the forest, and thus it has to honour and maintain every form of life, which grows independently, in its own sacred autonomy.

Does this mean that the government has no right *whatever* of interference in these autonomous spheres of life? Not at all.

It possesses the threefold right and duty: 1. Whenever different spheres clash, to compel mutual regard for the boundary-lines of each; 2. To defend individuals and the weak ones, in those spheres, against the abuse of power of the rest; and 3. To coerce all together to bear *personal* and *financial* burdens for the maintenance of the natural unity of the State. The decision cannot, however, in these cases, *unilaterally* rest with the magistrate. The Law here has to indicate the rights of each, and the rights of the citizens over their own purses must remain the invincible bulwark against the abuse of power on the part of the government.

And here exactly lies the starting-point for that coöperation of the sovereignty of the government, with the sovereignty in the social sphere, which finds its regulation in the Constitution. According to the order of things, in his time, this became to Calvin the doctrine of the "magistratus inferiores". Knighthood, the rights of the city, the rights of guilds and much more, led then to the self-assertion of *social* "States", with their own civil authority; and so Calvin wished the law to be made by the coöperation of these with the High magistrates.

Since that time these medieval relations, which in part arose from the feudal-system, have become totally antiquated. These corporations or social orders are now no longer invested with ruling power, their place is taken by Parliament, or whatever name the general house of representatives may bear in different countries, and now it remains the duty of those Assemblies to maintain the popular rights and liberties, of all and in the name of all, *with* and if need be *against* the government. A united defence which was preferred to individual resistance, both to simplify the construction and operation of State institutions and to accelerate their functions.

But in whatever way the form may be modified, it remains essentially the old Calvinistic plan, to assure to the people, in all its classes and orders, in all its

circles and spheres, in all its corporations and independent institutions, a legal and orderly influence in
the making of the law and the course of government,
in a healthy democratic sense. And the only difference
of opinion is yet on the important question, whether
we shall continue in the now prevailing solution of the
special rights of those social spheres in the *individual*
right of franchise; or whether it is desirable to place
by its side a *corporative* right of franchise, which shall
enable the different circles to make a separate defence.
At present a new tendency to organization reveals itself
even in the spheres of commerce and industry and not
less in that of labour, and even from France voices, like
that of Benoît, arise, which clamour for the juncture of
the right of franchise with these organizations.

I for one, would welcome such a move, provided its
application were not onesided, much less exclusive; but
I may not linger over these side issues. Let it suffice
to have shown, that Calvinism protests against State-
omnipotence; against the horrible conception that no
right exists above and beyond existing laws; and against
the pride of absolutism, which recognizes no constitutional rights, except as the result of princely favour.

These three representations, which find so dangerous
a nourishment in the ascendency of Pantheism, are death
to our civil liberties. And Calvinism is to be praised
for having built a dam across this absolutistic stream,
not by appealing to popular force, nor to the hallucina-
tion of human greatness, but by deducing those rights
and liberties of social life from the same source, from
which the high authority of the government flows—

even the *absolute sovereignty of God*. From this *one* source, in God, *sovereignty in the individual sphere*, in the family and in every social circle, is just as directly derived as the *supremacy of State-authority*. These two must therefore come to an understanding, and both have the same sacred obligation to maintain their God-given sovereign authority and to make it subservient to the majesty of God.

A people therefore which abandons to State Supremacy the right of the family, or a University which abandons to it the rights of science, is just as guilty before God, as a nation which lays its hands upon the rights of the magistrates. And thus the struggle for liberty is not only declared permissible, but is made a duty for each individual in his own sphere. And this not as was done in the French Revolution, by setting God aside and by placing man on the throne of God's Omnipotence; but on the contrary, by causing all men, the magistrates included, to bow in deepest humility before the majesty of God Almighty.

As third and last part of this lecture, the discussion remains of a question yet more difficult than the previous one, namely how we must conceive of *the Sovereignty of the Church* in the State.

I call this a difficult problem, not because I am in doubt as to the conclusions, or because I doubt your assent to these conclusions. For, as far as regards American life, all uncertainty in this respect is removed by what your Constitution at first declared—and has

later been modified in your Confessions—concerning the
liberty of worship and the coördination of Church and
State. And as far as I am personally concerned, more
than a quarter of a century ago I wrote above my
Weekly paper the motto—"A free Church in a free
State." In a hard struggle this motto has ever been lifted
on high by me, and our Netherland churches also are
about to reconsider the article in our Confession which
touches on this matter.

The difficulty of the problem lies elsewhere. It lies
in the pile and fagots of Servetus. It lies in the attitude
of the Presbyterians toward the Independents. It lies in
the restrictions of liberty of worship and in the "civil
disabilities", under which for centuries even in the Netherlands the Roman Catholics have suffered. The difficulty
lies in the fact that an article of our old Calvinistic
Confession of Faith entrusts to the government the
task, "of defending against and of extirpating every form
of idolatry and false religion and to protect the sacred
service of the Church." The difficulty lies in the unani-
mous and uniform advice of Calvin and his epigonies, who
demanded intervention of the government in the matter
of religion.

The accusation is therefore a natural one that, by
choosing in favour of liberty of religion, we do not pick up
the gauntlet for Calvinism, but that we directly oppose it.

In order to shield myself from this undesirable
suspicion, I advance the rule—that a system is not
known by what it has in common with other preceding
systems; but that it is distinguished by that in which it
differs from those preceding systems.

The duty of the government to extirpate every form of false religion and idolatry was not a find of Calvinism, but dates from Constantine the Great, and was the reaction against the horrible persecutions which his pagan predecessors on the Imperial throne had inflicted upon the sect of the Nazarene. Since that day this system had been defended by all Romish theologians and applied by all Christian princes. In the time of Luther and Calvin, it was an universal conviction that that system was the true one. Every famous theologian of the period, Melanchthon first of all, approved of the death by fire of Servetus; and the scaffold, which was erected by the Lutherans at Leipzig for Krell, the thorough Calvinist, was infinitely more reprehensible, when looked at from a Protestant standpoint.

But whilst the Calvinists, in the age of the Reformation, yielded their victims, by tens of thousands, to the scaffold and the stake, (those of the Lutherans and Roman Catholics being hardly worth counting), history has been guilty of the great and far-reaching unfairness of ever casting in their teeth this one execution by fire of Servetus, as a *crimen nefandum.*

Notwithstanding all this I not only deplore that one stake, but I unconditionally disapprove of it; yet not as if it were the expression of a special characteristic of Calvinism, but on the contrary as the fatal after-effect of a system, grey with age, which Calvinism found in existence, under which it had grown up, and from which it had not yet been able entirely to liberate itself.

. If I desire to know what in this respect must follow from the specific principles of Calvinism, then the

question must be put quite differently. Then we must
see and acknowledge that this system of bringing differences in religious matters under the criminal jurisdiction
of the government, resulted directly from the conviction
that the Church of Christ on earth could express itself
only in *one* form and as *one* institution. This *one*
church alone, in the Middle ages, was the Church of
Christ, and everything, which differed from her, was
looked upon as inimical to this one true church. The
government, therefore, was not called upon to judge, or
to weigh or to decide for itself. There *was* only one
Church of Christ on earth, and it was the task of the
Magistrate to protect that church from schisms, heresies
and sects.

But break that one Church into fragments, admit that
the Church of Christ can reveal itself in many forms,
in different countries; nay even in the same country,
in a multiplicity of institutions; and immediately everything which was deduced from this unity of the visible
church drops out of sight. And therefore, if it cannot
be denied that Calvinism itself *has* ruptured the unity
of the church, and that in Calvinistic countries a rich
variety of all manner of church-formations revealed
itself, then it follows that we must not seek the true
Calvinistic characteristic in what, for a time, it has
retained of the old system, but rather in that, which,
new and fresh, has sprung up from its own root.

Results have shown that, even after the lapse of three
centuries, in all distinctively Roman Catholic countries,
even in the South American Republics, the Roman
Catholic church is and remains the State-church, precisely

as does the Lutheran church in Lutheran countries. And the free churches have exclusively flourished in those countries which were touched by the breath of Calvinism, *i.e.*, in Switzerland, the Netherlands, England, Scotland and the United States of North America.

In Roman Catholic countries, the identification of the invisible and the visible church, under Papal unity, is still maintained. In Lutheran countries, with the aid of "cuius regio eius religio", the Court-confession has been monstrously imposed on the people as the land-confession; there the Reformed were treated harshly, they were exiled and outraged, as enemies of Christ. In the Calvinistic Netherlands, on the contrary, all those who were persecuted for religion's sake, found a harbour of refuge. There the Jews were hospitably received; there the Lutherans were in honour; there the Mennonites flourished; and even the Arminians and Roman Catholics were permitted the free exercise of their religion at home and in secluded churches. The Independents, driven from England, have found a resting place in the Calvinistic Netherlands; and from this same country the Mayflower sailed forth to transport the Pilgrim Fathers to their new fatherland.

I do not build therefore on subterfuge, but I appeal to clear historical facts. And here I repeat the underlying characteristic of Calvinism must be sought, not in what it has adopted from the past, but in what it has newly created. It is remarkable, in this connection, that, from the very beginning, our Calvinistic Theologians and jurists have defended liberty of conscience against the Inquisition. Rome perceived very clearly

how liberty of conscience must loosen the foundations
of the unity of the visible church, and therefore she
opposed it. But on the other hand it must be admitted that Calvinism, by praising aloud liberty of
conscience, has in principle abandoned every absolute
characteristic of the visible church.

As soon as in the bosom of one and the same people
the conscience of one half witnessed against that of the
other half, the breach had been accomplished, and placards
were no longer of any avail. As early as 1649 it was
declared that persecution, for faith's sake, was—"a spiritual murder, an assassination of the soul, a rage against
God himself, the most horrible of sins". And it is
evident that Calvin himself wrote down the premises
of the correct conclusion, by his acknowledgment that
against atheists even the Catholics are our allies; by
his open recognition of the Lutheran Church; and still
more emphatically by his pertinent declaration: "Scimus
tres esse errorum gradus, et quibusdam fatemur dan-
dam esse veniam, aliis modicam castigationem sufficere,
ut tantum manifesta impietas capitali supplitio plecta-
tur. 1) That is to say: "There exists a threefold departure from the Christian truth; a slight one, which
had better be left alone; a moderate one, which must
be restored by a moderate chastisement; and only
manifest godlessness must be capitally punished". I
admit that this is still a harsh decision, but yet a
decision in which in principle the *visible unity* is dis-
carded; and where that unity is broken, there liberty
will dawn as a matter of course. For here lies the

1) Tome VIII p. 516c Ed. Schippers.

solution of the problem: With Rome the system of persecution issued from the indentification of the visible with the invisible church, and from *this* dangerous line Calvin departed. But what he still persevered in defending was the identification of his Confession of the Truth with the absolute Truth itself, and it only wanted fuller experience, to realize that also this proposition, true as it must ever remain in our personal conviction, may never be imposed by force upon other people.

So much for the facts. Now let us put the theory itself to the test and look successively at the duty of the magistrate in things spiritual: 1°. towards *God*, 2°. towards the *Church*, and 3°. towards *individuals*. As regards the first point, the magistrates are and remain—"God's servants." They have to recognize God as Supreme Ruler, from Whom they derive their power. They have to serve God, by ruling the people according to *His* ordinances. They have to restrain blasphemy, where it directly assumes the character of an affront to the Divine Majesty. And God's supremacy is to be recognized, by confessing His name in the Constitution as the Source of all political power, by maintaining the Sabbath, by proclaiming days of prayer and thanksgiving, and by invoking His Divine blessing.

Therefore in order that they may govern, according to His holy ordinances, every magistrate is in duty-bound to investigate the rights of God, both in the natural life and in His Word. Not to subject himself to the decision of any church, but in order that he himself may catch the light which he needs for the knowledge of the Divine will. And as regards blasphemy, the *right* of the magistrate to restrain it rests in the God-consciousness innate in every man; and the *duty* to exercise this right flows from the fact that God is the Supreme and Sovereign Ruler over every State and over every Nation. But for this very reason the fact of blasphemy is only then to be deemed established, when the intention is apparent contumaciously to affront this majesty of God *as Supreme Ruler of the State.* What is then punished is not the religious offence, nor the impious sentiment, but the attack upon the foundation of public law, upon which both the State and its government are resting.

Meanwhile there is in this respect a noteworthy difference between States which are absolutely governed by a monarch and States which are governed constitutionally; or in a republic, in a still wider range, by an extensive assembly.

In the absolute monarch the consciousness and the personal will are *one*, and thus this one person is called to rule his people after his own personal conception of the ordinances of God. When on the contrary the consciousness and the will of many coöperate, this unity is lost and the subjective conception of the ordinances of God, by these many, can only be indirectly applied. But whether you are dealing with the will of a single individual, or with the will of many men, in a decision arrived at by a vote, the principal thing remains that the government has to judge and to decide independently. Not as an appendix to the Church, nor as its pupil. The sphere of State stands itself under the majesty of the Lord. In that sphere therefore an independent responsibility to God is to be maintained. The sphere of the State is not profane. But both Church and State must, each in their own sphere, obey God and serve His honour. And to that end in either sphere *God's Word* must rule, but in the sphere of the State only through the conscience of the persons invested with authority. The first thing of course is, and remains, that all nations shall be governed in a Christian way; that is to say, in accordance with the principle which, for all statecraft, flow from the Christ. But this can never be realized except through the subjective convictions of those in authority, according to their personal views of the demands of that Christian principle, as regards the public service.

Of an entirely different nature is the second question, what ought to be the relation between the government and the *visible Church*. If it had been the will of God to maintain the formal unity of this visible Church, this question would have to be answered quite differently from what is now the case. That this unity was originally sought is natural. Unity of religion has great value for the life of a people and not a little charm. And only narrow-mindedness can feel itself offended, by the rage of despair, wherewith Rome, in . the 16th century, fought for the maintenance of that unity. It can also be easily understood that this unity was originally established. The lower a people stands

in the scale of development, the less difference of
opinion is revealed. We see therefore that nearly all
nations begin with unity of religion. But it is equally
natural that this unity is split up, where the individual
life, in the process of development, gains in strength,
and where multiformity asserts itself, as the undeniable
demand of a richer development of life. And thus we
are confronted with the fact that the visible church has
been split up, and that in no country whatever the
absolute unity of the visible church can be any longer
maintained.

What then is the duty of the government?

Must it—for the question may be reduced to this,—
must it now form an individual judgment, as to which
of those many churches is the true one? And must it
maintain this one over against the others? Or is it the
duty of the government to suspend its own judgment
and to consider the multiform complex of all these
denominations, as the totality of the manifestation of
the Church of Christ on earth?

From a Calvinistic standpoint we must decide in
favor of the latter suggestion. Not from a false idea of
neutrality, nor as if Calvinism could ever be indifferent
to what is true and what false, *but because the government lacks the data of judgment*, and because every
magisterial judgment here infringes the *sovereignty of
the Church*. For otherwise, if the government be an
absolute monarchy, you get the "cuius regio eius religio"
of the Lutheran princes, which has ever been combated
from the side of Calvinism. Or if the government rests
with a plurality of persons, the Church which yesterday

was counted the false one, is to-day considered the true one, according to the decision of the vote; and thus all continuity of state-administration and church-position is lost.

Hence it is that the Calvinists have always struggled so proudly and courageously for the liberty, that is to say for the sovereignty, of the Church, within her own sphere, in distinction from the Lutheran theologians. In Christ, they contended, the Church has her own King. Her position in the State is not assigned her by the permission of the Government, but *jure divino*. She has her own organisation. She possesses her own office-bearers. And in a similar way she has her own gifts to distinguish truth from the lie. It is therefore her · privilege, and not that of the State, to determine her own characteristics as the true Church, and to proclaim her own confession, as the confession of the truth.

If in this position she is opposed by other churches, she will fight against these her spiritual battle, with spiritual and social weapons; but she denies and contests the right of every one whomsoever, and therefore also of the government, to pose as a power above these different institutions and to render a decision between her and her sister-churches. The government bears the sword which wounds; not the sword of the Spirit, which decides in spiritual questions. And for this reason the Calvinists have ever resisted the idea to assign to the ·government a *patria potestas*. To be sure a father regulates in his family the religion of that family. But when the government was organized, the family was not set aside, but remained; and the government received only a limited task, which is defined by the sovereignty in the individual sphere, and not least of all by the sovereignty of Christ in His Church. Only let us guard here against exaggerated Puritism and let us not refuse, in Europe at least, to reckon with the effects of historical conditions. It is an entirely different matter whether one puts up a new building, on a free lot, or whether one must restore a house which is standing.

But this can in no regard break the fundamental rule that the government must honour the complex of Christian churches, as the multiform manifestation of the Church of Christ on earth. That the magistrate has to respect the liberty *i. e.* the sovereignty of the Church of Christ in the individual sphere of these churches. That churches flourish most richly, when the government allows them to live from their own strength on the voluntary principle. And that therefore neither the Cœsaropapy of the Czar of Russia; nor the subjection of the State to the Church, taught by Rome; nor the "Cuius regio eius religio" of the Lutheran jurists; nor the irreligious neutral standpoint of the French revolution; but that only the system of a free Church, in a free State, may be honored from a Calvinistic standpoint.

The sovereignty of the State and the sovereignty of the Church exist side by side, and they mutually limit each other.

Of an entirely different nature, on the contrary, is the last question, to which I referred, namely the duty of the government, as regards the *sovereignty of the individual person.*

In the second part of this lecture I have already indicated that the developed man also possesses an individual sphere of life, with sovereignty in his own circle. Here I do not refer to the family, for this is a social bond between several individuals. I have reference to that, which is thus expressed by Prof. Weitbrecht: "Ist doch vermöge seines Gewissens jeder ein König, ein Souverain, der über jede Verantwortung erhaben is." 1) ("Every man stands a king in his conscience, a sovereign in his own person, exempt from all responsibility.") Or that, which Held has formulated in this way: "In gewisser Beziehung wird jeder Mensch supremus oder Souverain sein, denn jeder Mensch muss eine Sphäre haben, und hat sie auch wirklich, in welcher er der Oberste ist." 2) (In some respect every man is a sovereign, for everybody must have and has, a sphere of life of his own, in which he has no one above him, but God alone.) I do not point to this to over-estimate the importance of conscience, for whosoever wishes to liberate conscience, where God and His Word are concerned, I meet as an opponent, not as an ally. This however does not prevent my maintaining the sovereignty of conscience, as the palladium of all personal liberty, in this sense—that conscience is never subject to man but always and ever to God Almighty.

1) Weitbrecht, *Woher und Wohin.* Stuttgart 1877 p. 103.

2) Held, *Verfassungssystem* I p. 234.

This need of the personal liberty of conscience,
however, does not immediately assert itself. It does
not express itself with emphasis in the child, but only
in the mature man; and in the same way it mostly
slumbers among undeveloped peoples, and is irresistible
only among highly developed nations. A man of ripe
and rich development will rather become a voluntary
exile, will rather suffer imprisonment, nay even sacrifice
life itself, than tolerate constraint in the forum of his
conscience. And the deeply rooted repugnance against
the Inquisition, which for three long centuries would
not be assuaged, grew up from the conviction that its
practices violated and assaulted human life in man.
This imposes on the government a twofold obligation. In the first place, it must cause this liberty of
conscience to be respected by the Church; and in the
second place, it must give way itself to the sovereign
conscience.

As regards the first, the sovereignty of the Church
find its natural limitation in the sovereignty of the free
personality. Sovereign within her own domain, she has
no power over those who live outside of that sphere.
And wherever, in violation of this principle, transgression
of power may occur, the government has to respect
the claims on protection of every citizen. The Church
may not be forced to tolerate as a member one whom
she feels obliged to expel from her circle; but on the
other hand no citizen of the State must be compelled
to remain in a church which his conscience forces him
to leave.

Meantime what the government in this respect demands

of the churches, it must practise itself, by allowing to each and every citizen liberty of conscience, as the primordial and inalienable right of all men.

It has cost a heroic struggle to wrest this greatest of all human liberties from the grasp of despotism; and streams of human blood have been poured out before the object was attained. But for this very reason every son of the Reformation tramples upon the honour of the fathers, who does not assiduously and without retrenching, defend this palladium of our liberties. In order that it may be able to rule *men*, the government must respect this deepest ethical power of our human existence. A nation, consisting of citizens whose consciences are bruised, is itself broken in its national strength.

And even if I am forced to admit that our fathers, in theory, had not the courage of the conclusions which follow from this liberty of conscience, for the *liberty of speech*, and the *liberty of worship*; even if I am well aware that they made a desperate effort to hinder the spread of literature which they disliked, by censure and refusal of publication;—all this does not set aside the fact that the free expression of thought, by the spoken and printed word, has first achieved its victory in the Calvinistic Netherlands. Whosoever was elsewhere straightened, could first enjoy the liberty of ideas and the liberty of the press, on Calvinistic ground. And thus the logical development of what was enshrined in the liberty of conscience, as well as that liberty itself, first blessed the world from the side of Calvinism.

For it is true that, in Roman lands, spiritual and

political despotism have been finally vanquished by the French Revolution, and that in so far we have gratefully to acknowledge that this revolution also began by promoting the cause of liberty. But whosoever learns from history that the guillotine, all over France, for years and years could not rest from the execution of those who were of a different mind; whosoever remembers how cruelly and wantonly the Roman Catholic clergy were murdered, because they refused to violate their conscience by an unholy oath; or whosoever, like myself, by a sad experience, knows the spiritual tyranny, which liberalism and conservatism on the European Continent have applied, and are still applying, to those who have chosen different paths,—is forced to admit that liberty in Calvinism and liberty in the French Revolution are two quite different things.

In the French Revolution a civil liberty for every Christian *to agree with the unbelieving majority*; in Calvinism, a liberty of conscience, which enables every man to serve God, *according to his own conviction and the dictates of his own haert*.

FOURTH LECTURE.

CALVINISM AND SCIENCE.

In my fourth lecture allow me to draw your attention to the nexus between *Calvinism and Science.* Not, of course in order to exhaust in one lecture such a weighty subject. Four points of it only I submit to your thoughtful consideration; first, that Calvinism fostered and could not but foster *love for science;* secondly, that it restored to science *its domain;* thirdly, that it delivered science from *unnatural bonds;* and fourthly in what manner it sought and found a solution for the unavoidable *scientific conflict.*

First of all then: There is found hidden in Calvinism an impulse, an inclination, an incentive, to scientific investigation. *It is a fact,* that science has been fostered by it, and its principle demands the scientific spirit. One glorious page from the history of Calvinism may suffice to prove the fact, before we enter more fully upon the discussion of the incentive to scientific investigation found in Calvinism as such. The page from the history of Calvinism, or let us rather say of man-

kind, matchless in its beauty, to which I refer, is the
siege of Leyden, more than three hundred years ago.
This siege of Leyden was in fact a struggle between
Alva and Prince William about the future course of
the history of the world; and the result was, that in
the end Alva had to withdraw, and that William the
Silent was enabled to unfurl the banner of liberty
over Europe. Leyden, defended almost exclusively by
its own citizens, entered the lists against the best
troops of what was looked upon at that time as the
finest army of the world. Three months after the
commencement of the siege, the supply of food became
exhausted. A fearful famine began to rage. The apparently doomed citizens managed to live on dogs and
rats. This black famine was soon followed by the
black death or the plague, which carried off a third
part of the inhabitants. The Spaniard offered peace
and pardon to the dying people; but Leyden, remem-
bering the bad faith of the enemy in the treatment of
Narden and Harlem, answered boldly and with pride:
If it is necessary, we are ready to consume our left
arms, and to defend with our right arms our wives,
our liberty and our religion against thee, o tyrant.
Thus they persevered. They patiently waited for the
coming of the Prince of Orange, to raise the siege, . . .
but . . . the prince had to wait for God. The dikes of the
province of Holland had been cut through; the country
surrounding Leyden was flooded; a fleet lay ready
to hasten to Leyden's aid; but the wind drove the
water back, preventing the fleet from passing the
shallow pools. God tried his people sorely. At last

however, on the first of October, the wind turned towards the West, and, forcing the waters upward, enabled the fleet to reach te beleaguered city. Then the Spaniards fled in haste to escape the rising tide. On the 3rd of October the fleet entered the port of Leyden, and the siege being raised, Holland and Europe were saved. The population, all but starved to death, could scarcely drag themselves along, yet all to a man, limped as well as they could to the house of prayer. There all fell on their knees and gave thanks to God. But when they tried to utter their gratitude in psalms of praise, they were almost voiceless, for there was no strength left in them, and the tones of their song died away in grateful sobbing and weeping.

Behold what I called a glorious page in the history of liberty, written in blood, and if you now ask me, what has this to do with *science*, see here the answer: In recognition of such patriotic courage, the States of Holland did not present Leyden with a handful of knightly orders, or gold, or honour, but with a *School of the Sciences*,—the University of Leyden, renowned through the whole world. The German is surpassed by none in pride of his scientific glory, and yet no less a man than Niebuhr has testified, "that the Senate chamber of Leyden's University is the most memorable hall of science." The ablest scholars were induced to fill the amply endowed chairs. Scaliger was conveyed from France in a man-of-war. Salmasius came to Leyden under convoy of a whole squadron. Why should I give you the long list of names of the princes of science, of the giants in learning, who have filled Leyden with

10

the lustre of their renown, or tell you how this love for science, going forth from Leyden, permeated the whole nation? You know the Lipsii, the Hemsterhuizen, the Boerhaves. You know that in Holland were invented the telescope, the microscope and the thermometer; and thus empirical science, worthy of its name, was made possible. It is an undeniable fact, that the Calvinistic Netherlands *had* love for science and fostered it. But the most evident, the most convincing proof is doubtless found in the establishment of Leyden's University. To receive as the highest reward a University of the Sciences in a moment, when, in a fearful struggle, the course of the history of the world was turned by your heroism is only conceivable among a people, in whose very life-principle love for science is involved.

And now I approach the principle itself. For it is not enough to be acquainted with the fact, I must also show you why it is that Calvinism cannot but foster love for science. And do not think it strange, when I point to the Calvinistic dogma of predestination as the strongest motive in those days for the cultivation of science in a higher sense. But in order to prevent misunderstanding let me first explain what the term "science" here means.

I speak of human science as a whole, not of what is called among you "sciences", or as the French express it "sciences exactes". Especially do I deny, that mere empiricism in itself ever is perfect science.

Even the minutest microscopic, the farthest reaching telescopic investigation is nothing but *perception* with strengthened eyes. This is transformed into science, when you discover in the specific phenomena, perceived by empiricism, a universal *law*, and thereby reach *the thought*, which governs the whole constellation of phenomena. In this wise the special sciences originate; but even in them the human mind cannot acquiesce. The subject-matter of the several sciences must be grouped under one head and brought under the sway of one principle by means of theory or hypothesis, and finally Systematics, as the queen of sciences, comes forth from her tent to weave all the different results into one organic whole. It is true, I know, that Dubois Raymond's winged word *Ignorabimus* has been used by many, to make it seem impossible that our thirst for science in the highest sense will ever be quenched, and that Agnosticism, drawing a curtain across the background and over the abysses of life, is satisfied with a study of the phenomena of the several sciences; but some time ago, the human mind began to take its revenge on this spiritual vandalism. The question about the origin, interconnection and destiny of everything that exists, cannot be suppressed; and the *veni, vidi, vici*, wherewith the theory of evolution with full speed, occupied the ground in all the circles, inimical to the Word of God, and especially among our naturalists, is a convincing proof, how much we need unity of view.

How, now, can we prove that love for science in that higher sence, which aims at unity in our cognizance of

the entire cosmos, is effectually secured by means of
our Calvinistic belief in God's fore-ordination? If you
want to understand this you have to go back from
predestination to God's decree in general. This is not
a matter of choice; on the contrary, it *must* be done.
Belief in predestination is nothing but the penetration
of God's decree into your own personal life; or, if you
prefer it, the personal heroism to apply the sovereignty
of God's decreeing will to your own existence. It
means that we are not satisfied with a mere profession
of words, but that we are willing to stand by our
confession, in regard both to this life and the life to
come. It is a proof of honesty, unmovable firmness
and solidity in our expressions concerning the unity of
God's Will, and the certainty of His operations. It is
a deed of high courage, because it brings you under
the suspicion of high-mindedness. But if you now
proceed to the decree of God, what else does God's
fore-ordination mean, than the certainty that the existence and course of all things, *i. e.* of the entire cosmos, instead of being a plaything of caprice and chance,
obeys law and order, and that there exists a firm will
which carries out its designs both in nature and in
history. Now do you not agree with me, that this
forces upon our mind the indissoluble conception of
one all-comprehensive unity, and the acceptance of one
principle by which everything is governed. It forces
upon us the recognition of something that is general,
hidden and yet expressed in that which is special.
Yea, it forces upon us the confession, that there must
be stability and regularity ruling over everything. Thus

you recognize that the cosmos, instead of being a heap of stones, loosely thrown together, on the contrary presents to our mind a monumental building erected in a severely consistent style. Do you abandon this point of view, then it is uncertain at any moment, what is to happen, what course things may take, what every morning and evening may have in store for you, your family, your country, the world at large. Man's capricious will is then the principal concern. Every man may then choose and act every moment in a certain way, but it is also possible that he may do just the reverse. If this were so, you could count upon nothing. There is no interconnection, no development, no continuity; a chronicle, but no history. And now tell me, what becomes of science under such conditions? You may yet speak of the study of nature, but the study of human life has been made ambiguous and uncertain. Nothing but bare facts may then be historically ascertained, interconnection and plan have no longer a place in history. History dies away.

I do not for a moment propose to enter just now into a discussion about man's free will. We have no time for it. But it is a fact that the more thorough development of science in our age has almost unanimously decided in favor of Calvinism with regard to the antithesis between the unity and stability of God's decree, which Calvinism professes, and the superficiality and looseness, which the Arminians preferred. The systems of the great modern philosophers are, almost to one, in favor of unity and stability. Buckle's *History of the Civilization in England* has succeeded

in proving the firm order of things in human life with
astonishing, almost mathematical demonstrative force.
Lombroso, and his entire school of criminalists, place
themselves on record in this respect as moving on
Calvinistic lines. And the latest hypothesis, that the
laws of heredity and variation, which control the whole
organization of nature, admit of no exception in the
domain of human life, has already been accepted as
"the common creed" by all evolutionists. Though I
abstain at present from any criticism either of these
philosophical systems or of these naturalistic hypotheses, so much at least is very clearly demonstrated
by them, that the entire development of science in our
age presupposes a cosmos, which does not fall a prey
to the freaks of chance, but exists and develops from
one principle, according to a firm order, aiming at one
fixed plan. This is a claim, which is, as it clearly
appears, diametrically opposed to Arminianism, and in
complete harmony with Calvinistic belief, that there is
one Supreme will in God, the cause of all existing
things, subjecting them to fixed ordinances and directing
them towards a preestablished plan. Calvinists have
never thought that the idea of the cosmos lay in God's
foreordination as an aggregate of loosely conjoined
decrees, but they have always maintained, that the
whole formed one organic programme of the entire
creation and the entire history. And as a Calvinist
looks upon God's decree as the foundation and origin
of the natural laws, in the same manner also he finds
in it the firm foundation and the origin of every moral
and spiritual law; both these, the natural as well as

the spiritual laws, forming together one high order, which exists according to God's command, and wherein God's counsel will be accomplished in the consummation of His eternal, all-embracing plan.

Faith in such an *unity*, *stability* and *order* of things, personally, as predestination, cosmically, as the counsel of God's decree, could not but awaken as with a loud voice, and vigorously foster love for science. Without a deep conviction of this unity, this stability and this order, science is unable to go beyond mere conjectures, and only when there is faith in the organic interconnexion of the Universe, will there be also a possibility for science to ascend from the empirical investigation of the special phenomena to the general, and from the general to the law which rules over it, and from that law to the principle, which is dominant over all. The data, which are absolutely indispensable for all higher science, are at hand only under this supposition. Remember the fact, that in those days, when Calvinism cleared for itself a path in life, tottering semi-pelagianism had blunted this conviction of unity, stability and order, to such an extent that even Thomas Aquinas lost a great deal of his influence, while Scotists, mystics and Epicureans vied with one another in their endeavors to deprive the human mind of its steady course. And who is there who does not perceive, what entirely new impulse to undertake scientific investigations had to grow out of the new-born Calvinism, which with one powerful grasp brought order out of chaos, putting under discipline so dangerous a spiritual licentiousness, making an end to that halting between two or more

opinions, and showing us instead of rising and falling
mists, the picture of a powerfully-rushing mountain
stream, taking its course through a well regulated bed
towards an ocean which waits to receive it. Calvinism
has gone through many fierce struggles on account of
its clinging to the counsel of God's decree. Again and
again it seemed to be near the brink of destruction.
Calvinism has been reviled and slandered on account
of it, and when it refused to exclude even our sinful
actions from God's plan, because without it the programme of the order of the world would again be rent
to pieces, our opponents did not shrink from accusing
us of making God the author of sin. They knew not
what they did. Through evil report and good report
Calvinism has firmly maintained its confession. It has
not allowed itself to be deprived by scoff and scorn of
the firm conviction, that our entire life must be under
the sway of *unity*, *solidity* and *order*, established by God
himself. This accounts for its need of unity of insight,
firmness of knowledge, order in its world-view, fostered
among us, even in the wide circles of the common
people, and this manifest need is the reason, that a
thirst for knowledge was quickened, which in those
days was nowhere satisfied in a more abundant measure
than in Calvinistic countries. This explains why it is,
that in the writings of those days you meet with such
a determination, such an energy of thought, such a
comprehensive view of life. I even venture to say,
that in the memoirs of noble women of that century,
and in the correspondence of the unlettered, an unity
of world-view and life-view is manifest, which impressed

a scientific stamp on their whole existence. Intimately connected with this is also the fact that they never favoured the so-called primacy of the will. They demanded, in their practical life, the bridle of a clear consciousness, and in this consciousness the leadership could not be entrusted to humour or whim, to fancy or chance, but only to the majesty of the highest principle, wherein they found the explanation of their existence and to which their whole life was consecrated.

I now leave my first point, that Calvinism fostered *love for science*, in order to proceed to the second, that Calvinism restored to science *its domain*. I mean to say that cosmical science originated in the Graeco-Roman world; that in the middle ages the cosmos vanished behind the horizon to draw the attention of all to the distant sights of future life, and that it was Calvinism which, without losing sight of the spiritual, led to a rehabilitation of the cosmic sciences. If we were forced to choose between the beautiful cosmic taste of Greece with its blindness for things eternal, and the middle ages with their blindness for cosmical things, but with their mystic love for Christ, then certainly every child of God on his death-bed would tender the palm to Bernard of Clairvaux and Thomas Aquinas rather than to Heraclitus and Aristotle. The pilgrim, who wanders through the world without concerning himself about its preservation and destiny, presents to us a more ideal figure than the Greek worldling, who sought religion in the worship of Venus, or Bacchus,

and who flattered himself in hero-worship, debased his
honour as a man in the veneration of prostitutes, and
at last sank lower than the brutes in pederasty. Let
it be quite understood therefore that I do not in any
way over-rate the classical world, to the detraction of
the heavenly lustre which sparkled through all the haze
of the middle ages. But notwithstanding all this I
assert and maintain, that the one Aristotle knew more
of the cosmos than all the church-fathers, taken together;
that under the dominion of Islâm, better cosmic science
flourished than in the cathedral- and monastic-schools
of Europe; that the recovery of the writings of Aristotle
was the first incentive to renewed, though rather deficient
cosmic study; and that Calvinism alone, by means of
its dominating principle, which constantly urges us to
go back from the Cross to Creation, and no less by
means of its doctrine of *common grace*, threw open
again to science the vast field of the cosmos, now
illumined by the Sun of Righteousness, of Whom the
Scriptures testify, that in Him are hid all the treasures
of wisdom and knowledge. Let us pause then to consider
first that *general principle* of Calvinism and afterwards
the dogma of *"common grace"*.

All agree that the Christian religion is substantially
soteriological. "What must I do to be saved?" remains
throughout all the ages the question of the anxious
inquirer, to which above all else an answer must be
given. This question is unintelligble for those who
refuse to view time in the light of eternity, and who
are accustomed to think of this earth without organic
and moral connection with the life to come. But of

course, wherever two elements appear, as in this case the sinner and the saint, the temporal and the eternal, the terrestrial and the heavenly life, there is always danger of losing sight of their interconnection and of falsifying both by error or one-sidedness. Christendom, it must be confessed, did not escape this error. A dualistic conception of regeneration was the cause of the rupture between the life of nature and the life of grace. It has, on account of its too intense contemplation of celestial things, neglected to give due attention to the world of God's creation. It has, on account of its exclusive love of things eternal, been backward in the fulfilment of its temporal duties. It has neglected the care of the body, because it cared too exclusively for the soul. And this one-sided, inharmonious conception in the course of time has led more than one sect to a mystic worshipping of Christ alone, to the exclusion of God the Father Almighty, *Maker of heaven and earth*. Christ was conceived exclusively as the Saviour, and His *cosmological* significance was lost out of sight.

This dualism, however, is by no means countenanced by the Holy Scriptures. When John is describing the Saviour, he first tells us that Christ is the "eternal Word, by Whom all things are made, and Who is the life of men." Paul also testifies that all things were created by Christ and consist by Him;" and further, that the object of the work of redemption is not limited to the salvation of individual sinners, but extends itself to the redemption *of the world*, and to the organic reunion of all things in heaven and on earth under

Christ as their original head. Christ himself does not
speak only of the regeneration of the earth, but also
of a regeneration of the cosmos (Matth. 19 : 28). Paul
declares : "The whole creation groaneth waiting for the
bursting forth of the glory of the children of God."
And when John on Patmos listened to the hymns of the
Cherubim and the Redeemed, all honour, praise and thanks
were given to God, "Who has created the heaven and
the earth." The Apocalypse returns to the startingpoint
of Gen. I, 1.: "In the beginning God created the
heaven and *the earth*." In keeping with this, the final
outcome of the future, foreshadowed in the H. Scriptures,
is not the merely spiritual existence of saved souls, but
the restoration of the entire cosmos, when God will be
all in all under the renewed heaven on the renewed
earth. Now this wide, comprehensive, cosmical meaning
of the gospel has been apprehended again by Calvin,
apprehended not as a result of a dialectic process, but
of the deep impression of God's majesty, which had
moulded his personal life.

Certainly our salvation is of substantial weight, but
it cannot be compared with the much greater weight
of the glory of our God, Who has revealed His majesty
in His wondrous creation. This creation is His handiwork, and being marred by sin, the way was opened,
it is true for a still more glorious revelation in its
restoration, yet restoration is and ever will be the salvation of that which was first created, the theodicy of
the original handiwork of our God. The mediatorship
of Christ is and ever will be the burden of the grand
hymn of the tongues of men and the voices of angels,

but even this mediatorship has for its final end the glory of the Father; and however grand the splendour of Christ's kingdom may be, He will at last surrender it to God and the Father. He is still our Advocate with the Father, but the hour is coming, when His prayer for us will cease, because we shall know, in that day, that the Father loves us. Thereby of course Calvinism puts an end once and for all to contempt for the world, neglect of temporal and under-valuation of cosmical things. Cosmical life has regained its worth not at the expense of things eternal, but by virtue of its capacity as God's handiwork and as a revelation of God's attributes.

Two facts may suffice to impres you with the truth of this. During the terrible plague, which once devastated Milan, Cardinal Borromeo's heroic love shone brightly in the courage he manifested in his ministrations to the dying; but during the plague, which in the 16th century tormented Geneva, Calvin acted better and more wisely, for he not only cared incessantly for the spiritual needs of the sick, but at the same time introduced hitherto unsurpassed hygienic measures, whereby the ravages of the plague were arrested. The second fact, to which I draw your attention, is not less remarkable. The Calvinistic preacher Peter Plancius of Amsterdam was an enloquent sermonizer, a pastor unrivalled in his consecration to his work, foremost in the ecclesiastical struggle of his days, but at the same time he was the oracle of shipowners and sea-captains on account of his extensive geographical knowledge. The investigation of the lines of longitude and latitude

of the terrestrial globe formed in his estimation one
whole with the investigation of the length and breadth
of the love of Christ. He saw himself placed before
two works of God, the one in creation, the other in
Christ, and in both he adored that majesty of Almighty
God, which transported his soul into ecstacy. In this
light it is deserving of notice that our best Calvinistic
Confessions speak of two means, whereby we kwow
God, *viz*. the Scriptures *and Nature*. And still more
remarkable it is, that Calvin, instead of simply treating
Nature as an accessorial item, as so many Theqlogians
were inclined to do, was accustomed to compare the
Scriptures to a pair of spectacles, enabling us to deci-
pher again the divine Thoughts, written by God's Hand
in the book of *Nature*, which had become obliterated
in consequence of the curse. Thus vanished every
dread possibility, that he who occupied himself with
nature, were wasting his capacities in pursuit of vain
and idle things. It was perceived, on the contrary,
that for God's sake, our attention may not be with-
drawn from the life of nature and creation; the study
of the body regained its place of honour beside the
study of the soul; and the social organization of mankind on earth was again looked upon as being as
well worthy an object of human science as the congregation of the perfect saints in heaven. This also
explains the close relation existing between Calvinism
and Humanism. In as far as Humanism endeavored
to substitute life in this world for the eternal, every
Calvinist opposed the Humanist. But in as much as
the Humanist contented himself with a plea for a

proper acknowledgment of secular life, the Calvinist was his ally.

Now I proceed to consider the dogma of "*common grace*", that natural outcome of the general principle, just presented to you, but in its special application to *sin*, understood as corruption of our nature. Sin places before us a riddle, which in itself is insoluble. If you view sin as a deadly poison, as enmity against God, as leading to everlasting condemnation, and if you re-present a sinner as being "wholly incapable of doing any good, and prone to all evil," and on this account salvable only, if God by regeneration changes his heart, then it seems as if of necessity all unbelievers and unregenerate persons ought to be wicked and repulsive men. But this is far from being our experience in actual life. On the contrary the unbelieving world excels in many things. Precious treasures have come down to us from the old heathen civilization. In Plato you find pages which you devour. Cicero fascinates you and bears you along by his noble tone and stirs up in you holy sentiments. And if you consider your own surroundings, that which is reported to you, and that which you derive from the studies and literary productions of professed infidels, how much there is which attracts you, with which you sympathize and which you admire. It is not exclusively the spark of genius or the splendor of talent, which excites your pleasure in the words and actions of unbelievers, but it is often their beauty of character, their zeal, their

devotion, their love, their candor, their faithfulness and
their sense of honesty. Yea, we may not pass it over
in silence, not unfrequently you entertain the desire,
that certain believers might have more of this attract-
iveness, and who among us has not himself been put
to the blush occasionally by being confronted with
what is called the "virtues of the heathen"?

It is thus a fact, that your dogma of total depravity
by sin does not always tally with your experience in
life. Yet, if you now run to the opposite direction
and proceed from these experimental facts, you must
not forget, that your entire Christian confession falls
to the ground, for then you look upon human nature
as good and incorrupt; the criminal villains have to be
pitied as ethically-insane; regeneration is entirely superfluous in order to live honourably; and your imagination
of higher grace seems to be nothing else than playing
with a medicine, which often proves entirely ineffectual.
True, some people save themselves from this awkward
position by speaking of the virtues of unbelievers as
"splendid vices", and, on the other hand, by charging
the sins of believers to old Adam, yet you feel, yourselves, that this is a subterfuge, which lacks earnestness.

Rome tried to find a better way of escape in the
well known doctrine of the *pura naturalia*. Romanists
taught that there existed two spheres of life, the earthly
or the merely human here below, and the heavenly,
higher than the human as such; the latter offering
celestial enjoyments in the vision of God. Now,
Adam according to this theory, was well prepared by
God for both spheres, for the common sphere of life

by the nature He gave him, and for the extra-common by granting him the supranatural gift of original righteousness. In this wise Adam was doubly furnished for the natural as well as the celestial life. By the fall he lost the latter, not the former. His natural equipment for his earthly life remained almost unimpaired. It is true, human nature was weakened, but as a whole it remained in its integrity. Adam's natural endowments remained his possession after the fall. This explains to them why it is that fallen man often excels in the natural order of life, which is in fact merely human. You perceive that this is a system which tries to reconcile the dogma of the fall with the real state of things round about us, and on this remarkable anthropology is founded the entire Roman catholic religion. Two things only are faulty in this system, on the one hand it lacks the deep Scriptural conception of sin, and on the other it errs by the undervaluation of human nature to which it leads. This is the false dualism, to which a previous Lecture pointed, in the carnival. At that time the world is once more fully enjoyed, before one enters upon the *Caro vale*, but after the Carnival, in order to save the ideal, follows, for a short time, spiritual elevation into the higher sphere of life. For this reason the clergy, severing the earthly tie in celibacy, rank higher than the laity, and again, the monk, who turns away from earthly possessions also and sacrifices his own will, stands, ethically considered, on a higher level than the clergy. And finally the highest perfection is reached by the stylite, who, mounting his pillar, severs himself from everything earthly, or by the yet more

11

silent penitent who causes himself to be immured in
his subterranean cave. Horizontally, if I may use this
expression, the same thought finds embodiment in the
separation between sacred and secular ground. Everything uncountenanced and uncared for by the church,
is looked upon as being of a lower character, and
exorcism in baptism tells us, that these *lower* things
are really meant to be unholy. Now, it is evident that
such a standpoint did not invite Christians to make a
study of earthly things. Nothing but a study appertain-
ing to the sphere of heavenly things and contemplation
could attract those who under such a banner had mounted
guard over the sanctuary of the ideal.

This conception of the moral condition of fallen man
has been opposed in principle by Calvinism, on the one
hand by taking our conception of sin in the most
absolute sense, and on the other by explaining that
which is good in fallen man by the dogma of *common
grace*. Sin, according to Calvinism, which is in full
accord with the Holy Scriptures, sin unbridled and
unfettered, left to itself, would forthwith have led to a
total degeneracy of human life, as may be inferred from
what was seen in the days before the flood. But God
arrested sin in its course in order to prevent the complete
annihilation of his divine handiwork, which naturally
would have followed. He has interfered in the life of
the individual, in the life of mankind as a whole, and
in the life of nature itself by His common grace. This
grace, however does not kill the core of sin, nor does
it save unto life eternal, but it arrests the complete
effectuation of sin, just as human insight arrests the

fury of wild beasts. Man can prevent the beast from doing damage 1^0. by putting it behind bars; 2^0. he can subject it to his will by taming it; and 3^0. he can make it attractive by domesticating it, *e. g.*, by transforming the originally wild dog and cat into domestic animals. In a similar manner God by His "common grace" restrains the operation of sin in man, partly· by breaking its power, partly by taming his evil spirit, and partly by domesticating his nation or his family. Common grace has thus led to the result that an ungenerated sinner may captivate and attract us by much that is lovely and full of energy, just as our domestic animals do, but this of course after the manner of man. The nature of sin, however, remains as venomous as it was. This is seen in the cat, which, brought back to the woods, returns to its former wild state after two generations, and a similar experience has been made with regard to human nature, just now, in Armenia and Cuba. He who reads an account of the massacres of St. Bartholemew is easily inclined to place these horrors to the account of the low state of culture in those days, but behold! our nineteenth century has surpassed these horrors by the massacres in Armenia. And he who has read a description of the cruelties committed by the Spaniards in the 16th century in the villages and cities of the Netherlands against defenceless old men, women and children, and then heard the news of what occurred now in Cuba, cannot help acknowledging that, what was a disgrace in the 16th, has been repeated in the 19th century. Where evil does not come to the surface, or does not manifest itself in

all its hideousness, we do not owe it to the fact that
our nature is not so deeply corrupt, but to God alone,
Who by His "common grace", hinders the bursting
forth of the flames from the smoking fire. And if you
ask, how it is possible, that in such a way out of restrained evil something may come forth which attracts,
pleases and interests you, take then as an illustration
the ferry-boat. This boat is put in motion by the
current, which would carry it swiftly as an arrow down
stream and ruin it; but by means of the chain, to which
it is fastened, the boat arrives safely on the opposite
side, pressed forward by the same power, which would
otherwise have demolished it. In this wise God restrains
the evil, and it is He who brings forth good out of
evil; and meanwhile we Calvinists, never remiss in accusing our sinful nature, yet praise and thank God for
making it possible for men to dwell together in a well-
ordered society, and for restraining us personally from
horrible sins. Moreover we thank Him for bringing to
light all the talents, hidden in our race, developing,
by means of a regular process, the history of mankind,
and securing by the same grace, for his church on
earth, a place for the sole of her foot.

This confession, however, places the Christian in a
quite different position over against life. For then, in
his judgment, not only *the church*, but also *the world*
belongs to God and in both has to be investigated the
masterpiece of the supreme Architect and Artificer.

A Calvinist who seeks God, does not for a moment
think of limiting himself to theology and contemplation,
leaving the other sciences, as of a lower character, in

the hands of unbelievers; but on the contrary, looking upon it as his task, to know God in *all* his works, he is conscious of having been called to fathom with all the energy of his intellect, things *terrestrial* as well as things *celestial;* to open to view both the order of creation, and the "common grace" of the God he adores, in nature and its wondrous character, in the production of human industry, in the life of mankind, in sociology and in the history of the human race. Thus you perceive, how this dogma of "common grace" suddenly removed the interdict, under which secular life had lain bound, even at the peril of coming very near a reaction in favour of a one-sided love for these secular studies.

It was now understood, that it was the "common grace" of God, which had produced in ancient Greece and Rome the treasures of philosophic light, and disclosed to us treasures of art and justice, which kindled the love for classical studies, in order to renew to us the profit of so splendid an heritage. It was now clearly seen, that the history of mankind is not so much an aphoristic spectacle of cruel passions, as a coherent process with the Cross as its centre; a process in which every nation has its special task, and the knowledge of which may be a fountain of blessing for every people. It was apprehended, that the science of politics and national economy deserved the careful attention of scholars and men of thought. Yea, it was intuitively conceived, that there was nothing either in the life of nature round about us, or in human life itself, which did not present itself as an object worthy of investigation, which

might throw new light on the glories of the entire
cosmos in its visible phenomena and its invisible operations. And if on a different standpoint, progress in
thorough scientific knowledge on these lines often led
to pride and estranges the heart from God, we owe it
to this glorious dogma of common grace that in Calvinistic circles the most profound investigator never ceased
to acknowledge himself a guilty sinner before God, and
to ascribe to God's mercy alone, his splendid understanding of the things of the world.

Having proved that Calvinism has fostered *love for
science* and restored to science *its domain*, allow me
now in the third place to show in what manner it has
advanced its *indispensable liberty*. Liberty is for genuine
science, what the air we breathe is for us. This does
not mean that science is entirely untrammeled in the
use of its liberty and need obey no laws. On the
contrary, a fish lying on dry land is perfectly free, *viz.*,
to die and to perish, while a fish, which really shall be
free to live and to thrive must be entirely surrounded
by water and guided by its fins. In the same manner
every science has to keep up the closest connection
with its subject, and strictly to obey the claims of its
proper method; and only when strictly bound by this
double tie, can science move freely on. For the liberty
of science does not consist in licentiousness or lawless-
ness, but in its being freed from all unnatural bonds,
unnatural because they are not rooted in its vital prin-

ciple. Now in order fully to understand the position
Calvin took, we should abstain from any wrong conception of university-life in the middle ages. State
universities were not known in those days. The universities were free corporations, and in so far prototypes
of most of the universities in America. It was the
general opinion in those days, that science called into
existence a *respublica litterarum*, "a commonwealth of
learnéd men", which has to live upon its own spiritual
capital or to die of lack of talent and energy. The
encroachment upon the liberty of science in those days
came not from the State but from an entirely different
quarter. For ages two dominant powers, only, had
been known in the life of mankind, the *Church* and
the *State*. The dichotomy of body and soul was reflected
in this view of life. The Church was the *soul*, the
State the *body*; a third power was unknown. Church-
life was centralized in the *Pope*, while the political life
of the nations found its point of union in the *Emperor*,
and it was the endeavor to resolve this dualism into
a higher unity, that kindled the flames of the fierce
struggle for the supremacy of the imperial crown or
the papal tiara, as seen in the conflict between the
Hohenstaufen and the Guelphs. Since then, however,
science as a third power, thanks to the *Renaissance*,
had pushed itself in between them. Before the thir-
teenth century elapsed Science had found in the rising
university-life an embodiment of its own, and claimed
.an existence independent of pope and emperor.

The only remaining question was, whether this new
power also was to create an hierarchical centre, in order

to unveil itself as the third great potentate, at the side
of the pope and the emperor.

On the contrary the republican character of the university demanded the exclusion of all monarchical aspirations. But it was just as natural for Pope and
Caesar, who had partitioned among themselves the entire
domain of life, to watch with suspicion the growth of
a third, entirely independent power, and to try everything in order to subject the universities to their rule.
If all the then existing universities had taken a firm
stand such a plan would never have succeeded. But
as is often the case among free corporations, competition
allured the weaker to seek support from without and
so they turned for help to the Vatican. This compelled
the stronger Universities to follow, and rather soon the
favour of the Pope was universally coveted, in order to
secure special privileges. Herein is found the fundamental evil. In this wise Science surrendered its independent character. It was overlooked, that the intellectual
reception into, and the reflection from, our consciousness,
of the cosmos wherein all science consists, forms a
sphere entirely different from the Church. Now this
evil has been checked by the Reformation, and mastered
especially by Calvinism. Formally mastered, because in
the Church itself the monarchical hierarchy being abandoned, and under the monarchical authority of Christ
a republican and federal organisation having been introduced, a spiritual Church-head, whose task it would
be, to rule over universities, no longer existed for our
Calvinists. For Lutherans such a visible head was at
hand in the ruler of the land, whom they honoured as

"first Bishop", but nor for Calvinistic nations, which kept Church and State separate as two different spheres of life. A doctor's diploma, in their system, might not derive its significance from public opinion, neither from papal consent, nor from an ecclesiastical ordinance, but solely from the scientific character of the institution.

To this must be added a second point. Without regarding the Papal auspices over the University as such, the Church exercised pressure upon Science by harassing, accusing and persecuting the innovators on account of their expressed opinions and published writings. Rome did oppose, not only *in* the church, what was right, but also beyond its boundaries, the freedom of the word. Truth alone, not error, had the right to propagate itself in society and truth was expected to keep its ground, not by conquering error in honest conflict, but by arraigning it at the bar of justice. This impaired the liberty of Science, because it submitted scientific questions, which could not be settled by ecclesiastical jurisdiction, to the judgment of the civil Court. He who shrunk from conflicts, kept silence or submitted to circumstances; and he, who being of more heroic mettle defied opposition, was punished by having his wings clipped; and if he nevertheless tried to fly with clipped wings, had his neck wrung. He who published a book, betraying too bold opinions, was considered a criminal, and came at last in contact with the Inquisition and the scaffold. The right of free inquiry was unknown. Firmly believing, that everything knowable and worthy of being known, *was* known already, and known firmly

and well, the Church in those days had no idea of the
immense task, reserved for science, just awaking from
its mediaeval slumber, nor of the "struggle for life,"
which was to be the indispensable rule in the execution
of its task. The Church was unable to hail, in the dawn
of science, a rosy morn, heralding to the horizon the
rising of a new sun, but saw in its glittering rather the
smouldering sparks, which threatened to set the world
on fire; and therefore she considered herself justified and
in duty bound to quench this fire and to extinguish these
flames wherever an outbreak occurred. This position,
when we place ourselves back in those times, we can understand, but not without firmly condemning its underlying
principle, for it would have smothered nascent science
in its very cradle, if all the world had persisted in
favouring it. Glory, therefore, to Calvinism, which first
of all abandoned this pernicious position with effectual
results; theoretically by its discovery of the sphere of
common grace, and, before long, practically, by offering
a safe harbour to all who were caught in a storm
elsewhere. It is true, Calvinism, as always happens in
such cases, did by no means immediately understand
the full bearing of its opposition, for it began by
leaving the duty to extirpate error, untouched in its own
code, and yet the invincible idea, which was bound to
lead and in the course of time has led to freedom of
the word found its absolute expression in the principle,
that the Church has to retire to the domain of *particular*
grace, and that exempted from her rule lies the wide
and free domain of "*common* grace". The result of
this was that the penalties of criminal law were gradually

reduced to a dead letter, and that, to instance only one case, Des Cartes, who had to leave Roman Catholic France, found among the Calvinists of the Netherlands, of course a scientific antagonist in Voetius, but in the republic a safe retreat.

To this I must add that in order to cause science to flourish *a demand for science* had to be created, and to that end the public mind had to be made free. As long, however, as the Church stretched out her *velum* over the entire drama of public life, the state of bondage naturally continued, because the only object of life was to merit heaven and to enjoy as much of the world as the Church considered to be consistent with this main end. From this point of view it was unimaginable, that any one should be willing to devote himself with sympathy and with the investigators love to the study of our earthly existence. The seeking love of all was directed towards eternal life, and it could not be realized that Christianity, besides its yearning for eternal salvation, has to perform on earth, by divine commission, a grand task with regard to the cosmos. This new conception was first introduced by Calvinism when it cut at the root in the most absolute sense of every idea, that life on earth were ever destined to merit the blessedness of heaven. This blessedness, for every true Calvinist, grows out of regeneration, and is sealed by the perseverance of the saints. Where in this manner the "certainty of faith" supplanted the traffic of indulgences, Calvinism called Christendom back to .the order of creation: "Replenish the earth, subdue it and have dominion over everything that lives upon it." Christian life as a pilgrimage was not changed, but the

Calvinist became a pilgrim, who, while on his way to our eternal home, had yet to perform on earth an important task. The cosmos, in all the wealth of the kingdom of nature, was spread out before, under, and above man. This entire limitless field had to be worked. To this labour the Calvinist consecrated himself with enthusiasm and energy. For the earth with all that is in it, had, according to God's Will, to be subjected to man. Thus flourished, in those days, in my native country, agriculture and industry, commerce and navigation as never before. This new-born national life awakened new needs. In order to subdue the earth, a knowledge of the earth was indispensable, knowledge of its oceans, of its nature, and of the attributes and laws of this nature. And so it came to pass that the people itself, who had until now refrained from encouraging science, by a new and sparkling energy, suddenly called it into action, spurring it on to a sense of liberty, hitherto entirely unknown.

And now I approach my last point, *viz.*, the assertion, that the emancipation of Science must inevitably lead to a sharp *conflict of principles*, and that, for this conflict, also, Calvinism alone offered *the ready solution.* You understand, which conflict I have in view. Free investigation leads to collisions. One draws the lines on the map of life differently from his neighbour. The result is the origin of schools and tendencies. Optimists and pessimists. A school of Kant, and a school of Hegel. Among jurists the determinists oppose the moralists. Among medical men the homoeopaths oppose the allopaths. Plutonists and Neptunists, Darwinists and anti-Darwinists compete with one another in the natural sciences. Wilhelm van Humboldt, Jacob Grimm and Max Mueller form different schools in the domain of Linguistics. Formalists and Realists pick quarrels with one another within the classical walls of the philological temple. Everywhere contention, conflict, struggle, sometimes vehement and keen, not seldom mixed with personal asperity. And yet, although the energy of the difference of principle lies at the root of all these disputes, these subordinate conflicts are entirely put in the shade by the *principal conflict*, which in *all* countries perplexes the mind most vehemently, the powerful conflict between those who cling to the confession of the Triune God and His Word, and those who seek the solution of the world-problem in Deism, Pantheism and Naturalism.

Notice, that I do not speak of a conflict between faith and science. Such a conflict does not exist. Every science in a certain degree starts *from faith*, and, on the contrary, faith, which does not lead to science, is mistaken faith or superstition, but real, genuine faith it is not. Every science presupposes faith in self, in our self-consciousness; presupposes faith in the accurate working of our sences; presupposes faith in the correctness of the laws of thought; presupposes faith in something universal hidden behind the special phenomena; presupposes faith in life; and especially presupposes faith in the principles, from which we proceed; which signifies, that all these indispensable axioms,

needed in a productive scientific investigation, do not
come to us by proof, but are established in our judgment by our inner conception and *given with our self-
consciousness*. On the other hand every kind of faith
has in itself an impulse to speak out. In order to do
this it needs words, terms, expressions. These words
must be the embodiment of thoughts. Those thoughts
must be connected reciprocally not only with themselves but also with our surroundings, with time and
eternity, and as soon as faith thus beams forth in our
consciousness, the need of science and demonstration
is born. Hence it follows, that the conflict is, not
between faith and science, but between the assertion,
that the cosmos, as it exists to-day is either in a
normal or *abnormal* condition. If it is *normal*, then
it moves by means of an eternal evolution from its
potencies to its ideal. But if the cosmos in its present
condition is *abnormal*, then a *disturbance* has taken
place in the past, and only a *regenerating* power can
warrant it the final attainment of its goal. This, and
no other is the principal antithesis, which separates
the thinking minds in the domain of Science into two
opposite battle-arrays.

The *Normalists* refuse to reckon with other than
natural data, do not rest until they have found an
identical interpretation of all phenomena, and oppose
with the utmost vigour, at every turn of the line, all
attempts to break or to check the logical inferences of
cause and effect. Therefore, they also honour faith in
a *formal* sense but only as far as it remains in harmony with the general data of the human consciousness

and this be considered as normal. *Materially* however they reject the very idea of creation, and can only accept evolution,—an evolution without a point of departure in the past, and eternally evolving itself in the future, until lost in the boundless infinite. No species, not even the species *Homo sapiens*, originated as such, but within the circle of natural data developed out of lower and preceding forms of life. Especially no miracles, but instead of them the natural law, dominating in an inexorable manner. No sin, but evolution from a lower to a higher moral position. If they tolerate the Holy Scriptures at all, they do it on condition that all those parts, which cannot be logically explained as a human production be exscinded. A Christ, if necessary, but such a one as is the product of the human development of Israel. And in the same manner a God, or rather a Supreme Being, but after the manner of the Agnostics, concealed behind the visible Universe, or pantheistically hiding in all existing things, and conceived of as the ideal reflection of the human mind.

The *Abnormalists*, on the other hand, who do justice to relative evolution, but adhere to primordial creation over against an *evolutio in infinitim*, oppose the position of the Normalists with all their might; they maintain inexorably the conception of man as an independent species, because in him alone is reflected the image of God; they conceive of sin as the destruction of our original nature, and consequently as rebellion against God; and for that reason they postulate and maintain the miraculous as the only means to restore

the abnormal; the miracle of regeneration; the miracle
of the Scriptures; the miracle in the Christ, descending
as God with his own life into ours; and thus, owing to this
regeneration of the abnormal, they continue to find the
ideal norm not in the natural but in the Triune God.

Not faith and science therefore, but *two scientific
systems* or if you choose, two scientific elaborations,
are opposed to each other, *each having its own faith.*
Nor may it be said that it is here *science* which opposes
theology, for we have to do with two absolute forms of
science, *both* of which claim the whole domain of human
knowledge, and both of which have a suggestion about
the supreme Being of their own as the point of departure for their world-view. Pantheism as well as Deism
is a system about God, and without reserve the entire
modern theology finds its home in the science of the
Normalists. And finally these two scientific systems of
the Normalists and the Abnormalists are not relative
opponents, walking together half way, and, further on,
peaceably suffering one another to choose different paths,
but they are both in earnest, disputing with one another
the whole domain of life, and they cannot desist from
the constant endeavor to pull down to the ground *the
entire edifice* of their respective controverted assertions,
all the supports included, upon which their assertions
rest. If they did not try this, they would thereby
show on both sides, that they did not honestly believe
in their point of departure, that they were no serious
combatants, and that they did not understand the
primordial demand of science, which of course claims
unity of conception.

A Normalist, who retains in his system the slightest possibility of creation, of a specific image of God in man, of sin as a fall, of Christ in so far as he transcends the human, of regeneration, as different from evolution, of the Scriptures, as bringing us real oracles of God,— is an amphibious scholar and forfeits the name of scientist. But on the other side, he, who, as Abnormalist, transforms creation to a certain extent into evolution; who does not see in the animal a protoplastic creature, made in the image of man, but man's origin; who surrenders the creation of man in original righteousness; and who moreover tries every way, to explain Regeneration, Christ, and the Scriptures as the result of merely human causes, instead of clinging with all the energy of his soul to *the Divine cause*, as dominating in all this over all human data, must as decidedly be banished from our ranks as an amphibious and unscientific man. The *normal* and the *abnormal* are two absolutely differing startingpoints, which have nothing in common in their origin. Parallel lines never intersect. You have to choose either the one or the other. But whatever you may choose, whatever you are as a scientific man, you have to be it consistently, not only in the faculty of theology, but in all faculties; in your entire world- and life-view; in the full reflection of the whole world-picture from the mirror of your human consciousness.

Chronologically, it is true, we Abnormalists, for many ages in succession, have been the speakers, hardly ever having been challenged, while our opponents had scarcely no opportunity to dispute our principles. With

the decay of the old heathen, and the rise of the
Christian world-view, the general conviction soon took
deep root among all students, that everything has been
created by God, that the species of beings have been
brought into existence by special creative acts, and that
among these species of beings man has been created
as image-bearer of God in original righteousness; further, that the original harmony has been broken by
intervening sin; and that, in order to restore this abnormal state of affairs to its primitive condition, God
introduced the abnormal means of Regeneration, of
Christ as our Mediator and of the Holy Scriptures.
There were of course through all ages even in large
numbers, scoffers, who derided these facts, and indifferent
people, who took no interest in them; but the very
few, who during ten centuries scientifically opposed this
universal conviction, you may count at once on your
fingers' end. The Renaissance doubtless favoured the
rise of an infidel tendency, which was felt even in the
Vatican, and Humanism created enthusiasm for Graeco-
Roman ideals; but granted, that after the close of the
middle ages, the opposition of the Normalists made a
beginning, it yet remains a fact, that the large host of
philologians, jurists, physicians and physicists, for centuries afterwards left untouched these foundations, on
which the very old conviction rested. It was during
the eighteenth century, that the opposition made a
change of front by leaving the circumference and taking
up a position at the center; and it was the newer philosophy which, for the first time, on a general scale,
set out with the declaration, that the principles of the

Christian world-view were utterly untenable. In this manner the Normalists first began to suspect, and then became conscious of their fundamental opposition. Every possible position, available in this reaction against the hitherto prevalent conviction, has been since that time by turn developed into a special philosophical system. These systems, divergent, if compared with each other, were however in perfect agreement in their denial of the abnormal. After these philosophical systems had secured the assent of the leading men, the several sciences followed, and were immediately solicitous to introduce the new hypothesis of an infinite normal process as the starting-point of their special investigations in the domains of jurisprudence, medicine, natural science and history.

Then for a moment surely, public opinion was stupefied with sudden fright, but since the mass of the people lacked *personal* faith, this superficial reluctance was only of short duration. Within a quarter of a century the life-view of the Normalists had conquered in a literal sense the world in its leading centre. And only he, who adhered to the abnormalist view by virtue of his personal faith, refused to join in the chorus of those, who sang the praises of "modern thought", and at the first brunt, felt inclined to anathematize all science, retiring to the tent of mysticism. It is true, for a short time theologians tried to defend their cause apologetically, but this defense might be compared to a man who tries to adjust a crooked window-frame, while he is unconscious of the fact that the building itself is tottering on its foundations.

This is the reason, why the abler theologians, especially in Germany, imagined, that the best thing to do
would be to avail themselves of one or the other of
these philosophical systems as a prop to sustain Christianity. The first result of this compound of philosophy
and theology was the so-called mediating theology,
which gradually became poorer and poorer in its theological, richer and richer in its philosophical part, until
at last modern theology lifted up its head and found
its glory in the attempt, to cleanse theology of its
abnormal character in such a thorough manner, that
Christ was transformed into a man, born as we are
born, who was not even entirely free of sin, and the
Holy Scriptures into a collection of writings, for the
most part pseudepigraphic and in every possible
manner interpolated and filled with myths, legends
and fables. The song of the Psalmist: "We see not
our signs; they have set up their ensigns for signs",
has been literally fulfilled by them. Christ and the
Scriptures included, every sign of the abnormal was
rooted out, and the sign of the normal process em-
braced as the only genuine criterion of truth. In this
result, I repeat what I have already stated, there is
nothing to surprise us. He, who subjectively looks
upon his inner being and objectively upon the world
around him as normal, *cannot* but speak as he does,
cannot reach a different result, and would be *insincere*
in his position as a scientific man, if he were to represent things in a different light. And therefore from a
moral point of view, not thinking for a moment of
such a man's responsibility in the judgment of God,

nothing can be said against his personal stand-point, provided that, thinking as he does, he shows the courage, to voluntarily leave the Christian church in all its denominations.

———————

If the character of the keen and unavoidable conflict is thus and not otherwise, behold then the unconquerable position which Calvinism points out to us in the strain and struggle, resulting from this conflict. It does not keep itself busy with useless apologetics; it does not turn the great battle into a skirmish about one of the outworks, but immediately goes back to *human consciousness*, from which every man of science has to proceed as *his* consciousness. This consciousness, just on account of the abnormal character of things, is not the same in all. If the normal condition of things had not been broken, consciousness would emit the same sound from all; but as a matter of fact, this is not the case. In the one the *consciousness of sin* is very powerful and strong, in the other it is either feeble or entirely wanting. In the one the *certainty of faith* speaks with decision and clearness as a result of regeneration, the other does not even understand what it is. So also in the one the *Testimonium Spiritus Sancti* resounds loudly and in tones firm and strong, while the other declares, that he has never yet heard its testimony. Now, these three, consciousness of sin, certainty of faith and the testimony of the Holy Spirit, are constituent elements in the consciousness of every Calvinist. They form its immediate contents. Without these

three self-consciousness does not exist with him. This
the Normalist disapproves, and, therefore, he tries to
force *his* consciousness upon us, and claims, that
our consciousness has to be identical with his own.
From his point of view nothing else could be expected.
For if he conceded that there might be a real difference
between his consciousness and ours, he would thereby
have admitted a break in the normal condition of things.
We, on the contrary, do not claim, that *our* consciousness shall be found in *him*. It is true, Calvin maintains, that there is hidden in the heart of every man a
"religious seed",—*semen religionis*, and that the "God-
feeling",—*sensus divinitatis*, confessed or unconfessed,
in moments of intense mental strain, causes the soul to
tremble, but it is no less true, that it is just his system,
which teaches that human consciousness in a man who
believes and in a man who disbelieves, cannot agree,
but that on the contrary disagreement is inevitable.
He, who is not born again, cannot have a substantial
knowledge of sin, and he, who is not converted, cannot
possess certainty of faith; he who lacks the Testimonium
Spiritus Sancti, cannot believe in the Holy Scriptures,
and all this according to the thrilling saying of Christ
himself: "Except a man be born again, he *cannot see*
the kingdom of God"; and also according to the saying
of the apostle: "The natural man *receiveth not* the
things of the spirit of God". Calvin, however, does not
excuse unbelievers on this account. The day will come,
when they will be convinced in their own conscience.
But with regard to the *present* condition of things we,
of course, have to acknowledge *two kinds of human*

consciousness: that of the regenerate and the unregenerate; and these two cannot be identical. In the one
is found what is lacking in the other. The one is
unconscious of a break and clings accordingly to the
normal; the other has an experience both of a break
and of a change, and thus possesses in his consciousness
the knowledge of the *abnormal.* If, therefore, it be
true that man's own consciousness is his *primum-
verum,* and hence must be also the starting-point for
every scientist, then the logical conclusion is, that it
is an impossibility, that both should agree, and that
every endeavor to make them agree must be doomed
failure. Both, as honest men, will feel duty bound to
erect such a scientific edifice for the whole cosmos,
which is in harmony with the fundamental data, given
in their own self-consciousness.

You perceive immediately, how radical and fundamental
this Calvinistic solution of the perplexing problem is;
Science is not undervalued or pushed aside, but postulated
for the cosmos as a whole and all its parts. The
claim is maintained, that your science has to form a
complete whole. And the difference between the science
of the Normalists and Abnormalists is not founded
upon any differing result of investigation, but upon the
undeniable difference, which distinguishes the self-consciousness of the one from that of the other. *Free
science* is the stronghold we defend against the attack
of her tyrannical twin-sister. The Normalist tries to
do us violence even in our own consciousness. He
tells us, that our self-consciousness must needs be uniform
with his own, and that every thing else we imagine we

find in ours, stands condemned as self-delusion. In other words, the Normalist wishes to wrest from us the very thing, which, in our self-consciousness, is the highest and holiest gift, for which a continual stream of gratitude wells up from our hearts to God. He calls a lie in our own souls that which is more precious and certain to us than our life. With royal pride our consciousness of faith, and the indignation of our heart rise up against all this. We resign ourselves to the fate of being slighted and oppressed in the world, but we refuse to be dictated to by any one in the sanctuary of our heart. We do not assail the liberty of the Normalist to build a well construed science from the premises of his own consciousness, but our right and liberty to do the same thing we are determined to defend, if needs be, at any cost.

The parts are now exchanged. Not so very long ago the principal positions of Abnormalism were looked upon as axioms for all sciences in almost all universities, and the few Normalists, who at that time opposed the principle of their antagonists, found it difficult to find a chair. First they were persecuted, then outlawed, after that at the most tolerated. But at present they are the masters of the situation. controll all influence, fill ninety per cent of all professorial chairs, and the result is, that the Abnormalist, who has been forced out of the official house, is now obliged to look for a place, where he may lay down his head. Formerly we showed them the door, and now this sinful assault upon their liberty is by God's righteous judgment avenged by their turning us out into the street, and so it becomes the question, if the courage, the perseverance, the energy, which enabled them to win their suit at last, will be found now in a still higher degree, with Christian scholars. May God grant it! You cannot, nay, you even may not think of it, deprive him, whose consciousness differs from yours, of freedom of thought, of speech and of the press. That they, from their standpoint pull down everything that is holy in your estimation, is unavoidable. Instead of seeking relief for your scientific conscience in downhearted complaints, or in mystic feeling, or in unconfessional work, the energy and the thoroughness of our antagonists must be felt by every Christian scholar as a sharp incentive himself also to go back to *his* own principles in his thinking, to renew all scientific investigation on the lines of these principles, and to glut the press with the burden of his cogent studies. If we console ourselves with the thought, that we may without danger leave secular science in the hands of our opponents, if we only succeed in saving theology, ours will be the tactics of the ostrich. To confine yourself to the saving of your upper room, when the rest of the house is on fire, is foolish indeed. Calvin long ago knew better, when he asked for a *Philosophia Christiana*, and after all every faculty, and in these faculties every single science, is more or less connected with the antithesis of principles, and should consequently be permeated by it. As little may you seek your safety in shutting your eyes to the actual conditions of things, wherein so many Christians imagine they find a safe shield. Everything astronomers or geologists, physicists or chemists, zoologists or bacteriologists, historians or

archcologists bring to light has to be recorded,—detached
of course from the hypothesis they have slipped behind
it and from the conclusions they have drawn from
it,—but every fact has to be recorded by you, also,
as a fact, and as a fact that is to be incorporated as
well in your science as in theirs.

In order however to make this possible, university-
life has to be subjected again just as in the days when
Calvinism began its splendid career, to a radical change.
Of late university-life all over the world presumed, that
science grew up only from one homogeneous human
consciousness, and that nothing but learning and ability
determined whether you might claim a professorial chair
or not.   No-one thought, like William the Silent when
he founded the Leyden University over against that of
Leuven, of *two lines of universities*, opposed to one
another on account of radical difference of principle.
Since however the world-wide conflict between the Normalists and Abnormalists broke out in full force, the
need of a division of university-life began again to be
felt more generally on both sides.   The first in the
field were, (I speak only of Europe), the unbelieving
Normalists themselves, who founded the Université
Libre of Brussels.   Before this in the same Belgium
the Roman Catholic university of Louvain, in virtue
of old traditions, had been placed in opposition to the
neutral-universities of Liege and Ghent.   In Switzerland
a university arose at Freiburg, renowned, although yet
young, as an embodiment of the Roman Catholic prin-

ciple. In Great Britain the same principle is followed
in Dublin. In France, Roman Catholic faculties are
pitted against the faculties of the State institutions.
And also in the Netherlands Amsterdam saw the birth
of the Free University, for the general cultivation of
the sciences on the foundation of the Calvinistic principle.

If now, according to the demands of Calvinism, Church
and State withdraw, I do not say their liberal gifts,
but their high authority, from *university-life*, in order
that the university may be allowed to take root and
flourish in its own soil, then certainly the division,
which is already begun, will be accomplished of itself
and undisturbed, and in this domain also it will be
seen, that only a peaceful separation of the adherents
of antithetic principles warrants progress,—honest progress,— and mutual understanding. We here call upon
History as our witness. First, the emperors of Rome
tried to realize the false idea of *one State*, but the
division of their universal monarchy into a multitude
of independent nations was needed, to develop the hidden
political powers of Europe. After the fall of the Roman
Empire, Europe yielded to the enchantment of *one
world-Church*, until the reformation dispelled this delusion,
also, thus opening the way for a higher development
of Christian life. Nowhere else is this as clearly seen
as in the United States of America, where denominational multiformity gave a separate Church-embodiment
to every differentation of principle. In the idea of *one
Science* only, the old curse of uniformity is yet maintained. But of this also it may be prophesied, that
the days of its artificial unity are numbered, that it will

split up, and that in this domain also at least the
Roman Catholic, the Calvinistic and the Evolutional
principles will cause to spring up different spheres of
scientific life, which will flourish in a multiformity of
universities.   We must have systems in science, coherence
in instruction, unity in education.   That is only really
free, which, while it is strictly bound to its own prin·
ciple, has the power to free itself from all unnatural
bonds.   The final result, therefore, will be, thanks to
Calvinism, which has opened for us the way, that liberty
of science will also triumph at last; first by guaranteeing
full power to every leading lifesystem, to reap a scientific harvest from its own principle;—and secondly, by
refusing the scientific name to whatsoever investigator
dare not unroll the colours of his own banner, and
does not show emblazoned on his escutcheon in letters
of gold the very principle, for which he lives, and
from which his conclusions derive their power.

FIFTH LECTURE.

CALVINISM AND ART.

In this fifth lecture, which is the last but one, I speak of *Calvinism and Art.*

It is not the prevailing tendency of the day that induces me to do this. Genuflection before an almost fanatical worship of art, such as our time fosters, should little harmonize with the high seriousness of life, for which Calvinism has pleaded, and which it has sealed, not with the pencil or chisel in the *studio*, but with its best blood at the stake and in the field of battle. Moreover the love of art which is so broadly on the increase in our times, should not blind our eyes, but ought to be soberly and critically examined. It presents the fact, which is in every way explainable, that artistic refinement, thus far restricted to a few favored circles, now tends to gain ground among broader middle classes, occasionally even betraying its inclination to descend to the widest strata of lower society. It is the democratizing, if you like, of a life-utterance which hitherto recommended itself by its aristocratic allurements. And

though the really inspired artist may complain that,
with the majority, piano-playing is mere strumming,
and painting little more than daubing, yet, the exuberant feeling of having a share in the privileges of art
is so overwhelming, that the scorn of the artist is
preferred to the abandonment of art-training in education. To have laid a production of your own, however
poor, upon the altar of art becomes more and more
the characteristic of an accomplished civilization. Finally,
in all this the desire of enjoyment through ear and eye
expresses itself, especially by means of music and of
the stage. And if it cannot be denied that many court
these sensual pleasures in ways that are less noble and
too often sinful, it is equally certain, that in many instances this love of art leads men to seek enjoyment
in nobler directions and lessens the appetite for lower
sensuality. Especially in our great cities, stage-managers
are able to provide such first-rate entertainments, and
the easy means of communication between the nations
imparts such an international character to our best
singers and players, that the finest artistic enjoyments
are now brought for almost no price within the reach
of an ever-widening class. Besides, it is but fair to
concede that, threatened with atrophy by materialism
and rationalism, the human heart naturally seeks an
antidote against this withering process, in its artistic
instinct. Unchecked, the dominating influences of money
and of barren intellectualism would reduce the life of
the emotions to freezing-point. And, unable to grasp
the holier benefits of religion, the mysticism of the
heart reacts in an art-intoxication. Hence, though I

do not forget that the real genius of art seeks the heights of isolation rather than the plains below, and that our age, so poor in the production of real creative art, is deemed to warm itself at the splendid glow of the past; yea, though I admit, that the homage of art by the profanum vulgus must necessarily lead to art-corruption, nevertheless, in my estimation, even the most injudicious aesthetical fanaticism stands far higher than the common race for wealth, or an unholy prostration before the shrines of Bacchus and Venus. In this cold, irreligious and practical age the warmth of this devotion to art has kept alive many higher aspirations of our soul, which otherwise might readily have died, as they did in the middle of the last century. Thus you see, I do not underestimate the present aesthetical movement. But what in the light of History should be discountenanced, is the mad endeavor to place it higher than, or even to make it of equal value with the religious movement of the 16th century; yet this is what I should be doing if I begged for Calvinism the favor of this new artistic movement. And therefore, when I plead the significance of Calvinism in the domain of art, I am not in the least induced to do so by this vulgarization of art, but rather keep my eyes fixed upon the Beautiful and the Sublime in its eternal significance, and upon art as one of the richest gifts of God to mankind.

Here, however, every student of history knows that I founder upon a deeply-rooted prejudice. Calvin, it is said, was personally devoid of the artistic instinct, and Calvinism which in the Netherlands proved guilty of

Iconoclasm, cannot but be incapable either of artistic
development or of real, noteworthy art-production. A
brief word therefore about this strong prejudice is here
in order. Without putting too high an estimate upon
his: "Wer nicht liebt Weib, Wein und Gesang", it is
beyond dispute that Luther was more artistically dis-
posed than Calvin; but what does this prove? Will
you deny Hellenism its artistic laurels because, devoid
of all sense of the beautiful, Socrates boasted of the
beauty of his giant nose because it allowed his breath
to pass more freely? Do the writings of John, Peter
and Paul, the three pillars of the Christian Church,
in a single word betray any special appreciation of
artistic life? Yea, be it asked reverently, is there
any instance, in the Gospels, of Christ ever pleading
for art as such, or seeking its enjoyment? And when
these questions one by one, must be answered in the
negative, have you therefore the right to deny the
fact that Christianity as such has been of an almost
invaluable significance to the development of art? And
if not, why then would you accuse Calvinism on the
mere ground that Calvin personally had little feeling
for art? And when you speak of the Iconoclasm of the
Beggars, should you forget that in the 8th century in
the midst of the artistic and beautiful Grecian world
the manly spirit of Leo Isaurus instigated a still more
violent Iconoclasm? and should therefore the honour be
denied to Byzantianism of having produced the finest
monuments? Do you ask for still further proof to the
contrary? Well, more sharply even than Leo Isaurus in
the 8th century or the Netherland's Beggars in the 16th

century, did Mahomed in his Khorân militate against
images of all kinds, but will this justify the charge
that the Alhambra in Grenada and the Alcazar at
Seville are no wonderfully beautiful products of architectural art?

We must not forget that the artistic instinct is an
universal human phenomenon, but that in connection
with national types, climates and countries, the development of that artistic instinct is most unequally divided
among the nations. Who will look for a development
of art in Iceland, and who on the other hand will not
scent it, if I may so express myself, amidst the luxury
of nature in the Levant? Is it then a matter of surprise
that the South of Europe was more favorable for the
development of this artistic instinct than the North?
And when History shows that Calvinism was most
widely received by the peoples of the North, does it
prove aught against Calvinism, that in nations, living
in a colder climate and of poorer natural surroundings,
it was not able to quicken an artistic life such as
flourished among the Southern nations? Because Calvinism preferred a worship of God in spirit and in truth,
to sacerdotal wealth, it has been accused by Rome of
being devoid of an appreciation of art, and because it
disapproved of a woman debasing herself as an artist's
model or casting away her honour in the ballet, its
moral seriousness has clashed with the sensualism of
those who deemed no sacrifice too sacred for the Goddess
of Art. All this, however, concerns only the place
which art has to occupy in the sphere of life, and the
boundaries of its domain, but does not touch art itself.

13

To view therefore from a higher platform the significance of Calvinism to art, follow me in the investigation
of these three points: 1. why Calvinism was not allowed
to develop *an art-style of its own*; 2. what flows from
its principle for *the nature of art*; and 3. what it has
actually done for its *advancement*.

All would be well, if only Calvinism had developed
an architectural style of its own. Just as the Parthenon
is boasted of at Athens, the Pantheon at Rome, the
Saint Sophia at Byzantium, the Cathedral at Cologne,
or the Saint Peter's at the Vatican, so also ought Calvinism to be able to exhibit an impressive structure,
embodying all the fulness of its ideal. And that it did
not do this is considered sufficient proof of its artistic
poverty. Of course Calvinism is understood as having
tried to ascend to the same artistic luxury, but is censured as having proved unable to accomplish it; its
barren inflexibility being the obstacle that prevented every
higher aesthetical development. And when the humanist
boasts of the classic art of old Hellas, the Greek Church
of the Byzantian, and Rome of its Gotic Cathedral,
then Calvinism is looked upon as standing perplexed
by the painful charge of having lessened the fulness of
human life. Now in opposition to this thoroughly unfair
accusation, I maintain, that for the very reason of its
higher principle Calvinism was not allowed to develop
such an architectural style of its own. I was bound in
this connection to put architecture to the front, because
both in classic and in so-called Christian art the abso-

lute and all-embracing production of art was exhibited in architecture, all the other departments of art finally adapting themselves to the temple, church, mosque or pagoda. Scarcely a single art-style can be mentioned which dit not arise from the centre of divine worship and which dit not seek the realization of its ideals in the sumptuous structure for that worship. This was the thriving of an impulse which in itself was noble. Art derived her richest motives from Religion. The religious passion was the gold-mine, which financially rendered her boldest conceptions possible. For the realisation of her conceptions in this holy domain she found not only the narrow circle of artlovers, but also the whole nation at her feet. Divine worship furnished the tie that united the separated arts. And what tells more still, by this connexion with the Eternal, art received its inner unity and its ideal consecration. And this explains the fact that, whatever the palace and the stage may have done for the development of art, it was always the sanctuary by which it was impressed with the stamp of a special character and to which it was indebted for a creative style. Art-style and the style of worship coincided. Now of course, if this wedding of art-inspired worship, with worship-inspired art be no intermediate stage, but the highest end to be obtained, then it must frankly be confessed that Calvinism cannot but plead guilty. If, however, it can be shown that this alliance of religion and art represents a *lower* stage of religious, and in general of human development, then it is plain, that in this very want of a special architectural style, Calvinism finds an even higher recommendation. Being

fully convinced that this in the case, I procced to account
for this conviction.

First then the aesthetic development of divine worship
carried to those ideal heights of which the Parthenon
and the Pantheon, the Saint Sophia and Saint Peter
are the stone-embroidered witnesses, is only possible at
that lower stage, in which the same form of religion
is imposed upon a whole nation, both by prince and
priest. In that case every difference of spiritual expression fuses into one mode of symbolical worship, and
this union of the masses, under the leadership of the
magistrate and the clergy, furnishes the possibility of
defraying the immense expense of such colossal struct-
ures, and of ornamenting and decorating them. In the
case, however, of a progressive development of the nations,
when individual character-traits split the unity of the
masses, Religion also rises to that higher plain where
it graduates from the symbolical into the clearly-
conscious life, and thereby necessitates both the division
of worship into many forms, and the emancipation of
matured religion from all sacerdotal and political guardianship. In the 16th century Europe was approaching,
though slowly, this higher level of spiritual development,
and it was not Lutheranism with its subjection of the
whole nation to the religion of the prince, but Calvinism
with its profound conception of religious liberty, which
initiated the transition. In every country where Calvinism has made its appearance, it has led to a multiformity
of life-tendencies, in has broken the power of the State
within the domain of religion, and to a great extent
has made an end of sacerdotalism. As a result of this,

it abandoned the symbolical form of worship, and refused, at the demand of art, to embody its religious spirit in monuments of splendor.

The objection that such a symbolic service had a place in Israel does not weaken my argument, it rather supports it. For does not the New Testament teach us that the ministry of shadows, naturally flourishing under the old dispensation, under the dispensation of fulfilled prophecy is "old and waxeth aged and is nigh unto vanishing away?" In Israel we find a state-religion, which is one and the same for the entire people. That religion is under sacerdotal leadership. And finally it makes its appearance in symbols, and is consequently embodied in the splendid temple of Solomon. But when this ministry of shadows has served the purposes of the Lord, Christ comes to prophecy the hour when God shall no longer be worshipped in the monumental temple at Jerusalem, but shall rather be worshipped in spirit and in truth. And in keeping with this prophecy you find no trace or shadow of art for worship in all the apostolic literature. Aaron's visible priesthood on earth gives place to the invisible High-priesthood after the order of Melchizedek in Heaven. The purely spiritual breaks through the nebula of the symbolical.

· My second proof is that this agrees entirely with the higher relation between *Religion* and *Art*. Here I appeal to Hegel and Von Hartmann who, both standing outside Calvinism, may be relied upon as being disinterested witnesses. Hegel says that art, which, at a lower stage of development, imparts to a still

sensual religion its highest expression, finally helps it
by these very means to cast off the fetters of sensuality;
for though it must be granted that at a lower level it
is only the aesthetical worship that liberates the spirit,
nevertheless, he concludes, "beautiful art is not its
highest emancipation", for that is only found in the
realm of the invisible and spiritual. And Von Hartmann even more emphatically declares that: Originally
Divine worship appeared inseparably united to art,
because, at the lower stage, Religion is still inclined to
lose itself in the aesthetic form. At that period, all
the arts, he says, engage in the service of the cult,
not merely music, painting, sculpture and architecture, but also the dance, mimicry and the drama.
The more, on the other hand, Religion develops
into spiritual maturity, the more it will extricate
itself from art's bandages, because art always remains
incapable of expressing the very essence of Religion.
And the final result of this historic process of separation,
he concludes, must be, that Religion, when fully matured,
will rather entirely abstain from the stimulant by which
aesthetic pseudo-emotion intoxicated it, in order to concentrate itself wholly and exclusively upon the quickening
of those emotions which are *purely religious.*"

And both Hegel and Von Hartmann are correct in
this fundamental thought. Religion and Art have each
a life-sphere of their own; these may at first be scarcely
distinguishable from each other and therefore closely
intertwined, but, with a richer development, these two
spheres necessarily separate. Looking at two babies in
a cradle you can scarcely tell which is boy or girl, but

when, having reached the years of maturity, they stand
before you, as man and woman, you see them both
with forms, and traits, and modes of expression, peculiarly their own. And so, arrived at their highest development, both Religion and Art demand an independent existence, and the two stems which at first were
intertwined and seemed to belong to the same plant,
now appear to spring from a root of their own. This
is the process from Aäron to Christ, from Bezaleël and
Aholiab to the Apostles. And, by virtue of that same
process, Calvinism occupies a higher standpoint in the
16th century than Romanism could reach. Consequently
Calvinism was neither able, nor even permitted, to develop an art-style of its own from its religious principle.
To have done this would have been to slide back to
a lower level of religious life. On the contrary, its
nobler effort must be to release religion and divine
worship more and more from its sensual form and to
encourage its vigorous spirituality. This it was enabled
to do because of the powerful pulsebeat by which at
that time the religious life coursed through the arteries
of mankind.* And the fact that in these days, our Calvinistic churches are deemed cold and *unheimisch*, and a
reintroduction of the symbolical in our places of worship
is longed for, we owe to the sad reality that the pulsebeat of the religious life in our times is so much fainter
than it was in the days of our martyrs. But so far
from borrowing from this the right of redescending to
a lower level of religion, this faintness of the religious
life ought to inspire the prayer for a mightier inworking of the Holy Spirit. Second childhood, in your

old age, is a painful, retrograde movement. The man who fears God, and whose faculties remain clear and unimpaired, does not on the brink of age return to the playthings of his infancy.

One more objection might maintain itself after this demonstration, and that too I want to face. The question may be asked whether a really independent life-tendency should not create its own art-style, even if it developed itself as absolutely secular. Let the real meaning of the objection be well understood. It does not suggest that Calvinism if truly possessed of an aesthetic significance, should have given a certain direction to the practice of art, for the fact that Calvinism has truly done this will presently show itself. The point of this objection hits deeper, and puts the question: whether in the first place a secular art-style is conceivable; and in the second place, whether the creation of such a purely secular and dominating art-style could have been demanded of Calvinism. The answer I make to the first is: that in the history of art no record of the rise of such an all-embracing art-style independent of Religion, is to be found. Mark you, I do not here speak of a school of a single art, but of an art-style which puts a concentric impress upon all the arts together. To a certain degree it could be asserted of Roman art and of that of the Renaissance that, although devoid of a leading religious impulse, they nevertheless reached an all-sided revelation in art-forms. Speaking of architecture, the dome in Roman and Byzantian art is not an expression of a religious thought but of political energy. The dome symbolizes world-power, and, though it may be in a different sense, of the Renaissance also it must be confessed, that it did not take its rise in religion, but in the circles of civil and social life. Now the Renaissance will be considered more fully in the third part of this lecture, but with respect to the Roman art-style I here answer, first, that a style, which borrowed almost all its motives from Greek art can scarcely boast of an independent character; and secondly, that, in Rome, the State-idea had become so identified with the Religious idea, that when, in the period of the emperors, art reached its height of prosperity while sacrifices were burned to Divus Augustus, it is unhistorical to consider State and Religion any longer as being at that time separate spheres.

But, apart from this historic outcome, it may be questioned, whether such an all-embracing art-style ever *could* have originated outside of Religion. The rise of such a style demands a central motive in the mental and emotional life of a people, which shall dominate the whole existence from within, and which consequently carries its effect from this spiritual centre to its outermost circumference. Not of course as though a national world of art ever could be the product of intellectual thought. Intellectual art is no art, and the effort put forth by Hegel to draw art from thoughts, militated against the very nature of art. Our intellectual, ethical, religious and aesthetic life each commands a sphere of its own. These spheres run parallel and do not allow the derivation of one from the other. It is the central emotion, the central impulse, and the central animation, in the mystical root of our being, which seeks to reveal itself to the outer world in this fourfold ramification. Art also is no side-shoot on a principal branch, but an independent branch that grows from the trunk of our life itself, even though it is far more nearly allied to Religion than to our thinking or to our ethical being. If however it be asked how there can arise a unity of conception embracing these four domains, it constantly appears that in the finite this unity is only found at that point where it springs from the fountain of the Infinite. There is no unity in your thinking save by a well-ordered philosophical system, and there is no system of philosophy which does not ascend to the issues of the Infinite. In the same way there is no unity in your moral existence save by the union of your inner existence with the moral world-order, and there is no moral world-order conceivable but for the impression of an Infinite power that has ordained order in this moral world. Thus also no unity in the revelation of art is conceivable, except by the art-inspiration of an Eternal Beautiful, which flows from the fountain of the Infinite. Hence no characteristic all-embracing art-style can arise except as a consequence of the peculiar impulse from the Infinite that operates in our inmost being. And since this is the very privilege of Religion, over intellect, morality and art, that she alone effects the communion with the Infinite in our self-consciousness, the call for a secular, all-embracing art-style, independent of any religious principle, is simply absurd.

Understand that art is no fringe that is attached to the garment, and no amusement that is added to life,

but a most serious power in our present existence, and
therefore its principal variations must maintain, in their
artistic expression, a close relation with the principal
variations of our entire life; and since, without exception,
these principal variations of our entire human existence
are dominated by our relation to God, would it not
be both a *degradation* and *an underestimation* of art,
if you were to imagine the ramifications, into which
the art-trunk divides itself, to be independent of the
deepest root which all human life has in God?
Consequently no art-style has sprung from the Rationalism of the 18th century, nor from the principle
of 1789, and however grievous it may be to our
19th century, all her efforts to create a new art-
style of her own, have ended in perfect failure, and
then only do her artistic productions possess a real
charm when she allows herself to be inspired bij the
wonders of the past.

Thus by itself the possibility must be denied that a
proper art-style can originate independently of religion;
but even if this were otherwise, it would still be illogical,
and this was my second argument, to demand such a
secular tendency of Calvinism. For how can you desire
that a life-movement, which found the origin of its
power in the arraignment of all men and of all human
life before the face of God, should have sought the impulse, the passion and the inspiration for its life *outside*
of God in so exceedingly important a domain as that
of the mighty arts? There remains, therefore, no shadow of a reality in the scornful reproach that the non-
creation of an architectural style of its own is a conclusive

proof of Calvinism's artistic poverty. Only under the
auspices of its religious principle could Calvinism have
created a general art-style, and just because it had reached
a so much higher stage of religious development, its
very principle forbade it the symbolical expression of
its religion in visible and sensual forms.

Hence the question must be differently stated. And
this brings us to our second point. The question is not
whether Calvinism produced what, with its higher view-
point it was no longer allowed to create, *viz.*, a general
art-style of its own, but *what interpretation of the nature
of art flows from its principle.* In other words, is there
in the life- and world-view of Calvinism a place for
art, and if so, what place? Is its principle opposed to
art, or, if judged by the standards of the Calvinistic
principle, would a world without *art* loose one of its
ideal spheres? I do not speak now of the abuse,
but simply of the use of art. In every domain, life
is bound to respect the dimensions of this domain.
Encroachment on the domain of others is always un-
lawful; and our human life will only then attain its
nobler harmony when all its functions cooperate in just
proportion to our general development. The logic of
the mind may not scorn the feelings of the heart, nor
should the love of the beautiful silence the voice of
conscience. However holy Religion may be, it must
keep within its own bounds, lest, in crossing its lines,
it degenerate into superstition, insanity or fanaticism.
And, in the same way, the too exuberant passion for

art which laughs at the whispering of conscience, must
end in an unlovely discord quite different from what
the Greeks exalted in their *kalokagathos*. The fact,
for instance, that Calvinism arrayed itself against all
unholy play with woman's honour, and stigmatized every
form of immoral artistic enjoyment as a degradation,
lies therefore outside our scope. All this properly de-
nounces the abuse, while it carries no weight whatever
with the question of the lawful use. And that the
lawful use of art was not opposed, but encouraged and
even recommended, by Calvin himself, his own words
readily prove. When the Scripture mentions the first
appearance of art, in the tents of Jubal, who invented
the harp and organ, Calvin emphatically reminds us
that this passage treats of "excellent gifts of the Holy
Spirit." He declares that in the artistic instinct God
had enriched Jubal and his posterity with rare endowments. And he frankly states that these inventive
powers of art prove most evident testimonies of
the Divine bounty. More emphatically still, he declares, in his commentaries on Exodus, that "all the
arts come from God and are to be respected as
Divine inventions." According to Calvin, these precious things of the natural life we owe originally to
the Holy Ghost. In all Liberal Arts, in the most as
well as in the least important, the praise and glory of
God are to be enhanced. The arts, says he, have been
given us for our comfort, in this our depressed estate
of life. They react against the corruption of life and
nature by the curse. When his colleague, Prof. Cop,
at Geneva, took up arms against art, Calvin purposely

instituted measures, by which, as he writes, to restore
this foolish man to sounder sense and reason. The
blind prejudice against Sculpture, on the ground of the
Second Commandment, Calvin declares unworthy of
refutation. He exults in Music as a marvellous power
to move hearts and to ennoble tendencies and morals.
Among the excellent favors of God for our recreation
and enjoyment, it occupies in his mind the highest .
rank. And even when art condescends to become the
instrument of mere entertainment to the masses, he
asserts that this sort of pleasure should not be denied
them. In view of all this we may say, that Calvin
esteemed art, in all its ramifications, as a gift of God,
or, more especially, as a gift of the Holy Ghost; that
he fully grasped the profound effects worked by art
upon the life of the emotions; that he appreciated the
end for which art has been given, *viz.*, that by it we
might glorify God, and ennoble human life, and drink
at the fountain of higher pleasures, yea even of common
sport; and finally, that so far from considering art as
a mere imitation of nature, he attributed to it the noble
vocation of disclosing to man a higher reality than was
offered to us by this sinful and corrupted world.

Now if this implied nothing beyond the personal
interpretation of Calvin, his testimony would of course
have no conclusive value for Calvinism in general. But
when we observe that Calvin himself was not artistically developped, and that therefore he must have derived
this brief system of Aesthetics from his principles, he may
be credited with having expounded the Calvinistic consideration of art as such. To go direct to the heart of the quest-

ion, we begin with Calvin's last saying, *viz.*, that art reveals to us a higher reality than is offered by this sinful world. You are familiar with the question, already mentionned, whether art should imitate nature or should transcend it. In Greece grapes were painted with such accuracy that birds were deceived by their appearance and tried to eat them. And this imitation of nature seemed the highest ideal to the Socratic school. Herein lies the truth, all too often forgotten by idealists, that the forms and relations exhibited by nature are and ever must remain the fundamental forms and relations of all actual reality, and an art which does not watch the forms and motions of nature nor listen to its sounds, but arbitrarily likes to hover over it, deteriorates into a wild play of fantasy. But on the other hand all idealistic interpretation of art should be justified in opposition to the purely empirical, as often as the empirical confines its task to mere imitation. For then the same mistake is committed in art so often committed by scientists when they confine their scientific task to the mere observation, computation and accurate report of facts. For even as science has to ascend from the phenomena to the investigation of their inherent order, to the end that man, enriched by the knowledge of this order, may propagate nobler species of animals, flowers and fruits, than nature, herself, could produce, so also it is the vocation of art, not merely to observe every thing visible and audible, to apprehend it, and reproduce it artistically, but much more to discover in those natural forms the order of the beautiful, and, enriched by this higher kwowledge, to produce a beautiful

world that transcends the beautiful of nature. And this
is what Calvin asserted; *viz.*, that the arts exhibit gifts
which God has placed at our disposal, now that, as
the sad consequence of sin, the real beautiful has fled
from us.—Your decision here depends entirely upon
your interpretation of the world. If you are considering
the world as the realisation of the absolute good, then
there is none higher, and art can have no other vocation than to copy nature. If, as the pantheist teaches,
the world proceed, by slow processes, from the incomplete to perfection, then art becomes the prophecy of
a further phase of life to come. But if you confess
that the world once *was* beautiful, but by the curse
has become *undone*, and by a final catastrophy is to
pass to its full state of glory, excelling even the beautiful of paradise, than art has the mystical task of
reminding us in its productions of the beautiful that
was lost and of anticipating its perfect coming lustre.
Now this last-mentioned instance is the Calvinistic confession. It realized, more clearly than Rome, the hideous,
corrupting influences of sin; this led to a higher estimation of the nature of paradise in the beauty of original
righteousness; and guided by this enchanting remembrance, Calvinism prophesied a redemption of outward
nature also, to be realized in the reign of celestial glory.
From this standpoint, Calvinism honoured art as a gift
of the Holy Ghost and as a consolation in our present
life, enabling us to discover in and behind this sinful
life a richer and more glorious background. Standing
by the ruins of this once so wonderfully beautiful creation, art points out to the Calvinist both the still visible

lines of the original plan, and what is even more, the splendid restoration by which the Supreme Artist and Master-Builder will one day renew and enhance even the beauty of His original creation.

If thus, on this principal point, Calvin's personal interpretation agrees entirely with the Calvinistic confession, the same applies to the next point in question. If the Sovereignty of God is and remains, for Calvinism, its unchangeable point of departure, then art cannot originate from the Evil One; for Satan is, destitute of every creative power. All he can do is to abuse the good gifts of God. Neither can art originate with man, for, being a creature himself, man cannot but employ the powers and gifts put by God at his disposal. If God is and remains Sovereign, then art can work no enchantment except in keeping with the ordinances which God ordained for the beautiful, when He, as the Supreme Artist, called this world into existence. And further, if God is and remains Sovereign, then he also imparts these artistic gifts to whom He will, first even to Cain's, and not to Abel's posterity; not as if art were Cainitic, but in order that he who has sinned away the highest gifts, should at least, as Calvin so beautifully says, in the lesser gifts of art have some testimony of the Divine bounty. That artistic ability, that art-capacity, as such, can have room in human nature, we owe to our creation after the image of God. In the real world, God is Creator of everything; the power of really producing new things is His alone, and therefore He always continues to be the creative artist. As God, He alone is the original One, we are only

14

the bearers of His Image. Our capacity to create after Him and after what He created, can only consist in the *unreal* creations of art. So we, in our fashion, may imitate God's handiwork. We create a kind of cosmos, in our Architectural monument; to embellish nature's forms, in Sculpture; to reproduce life, animated by lines and tints, in our Painting; to transfuse the mystical spheres in our Music and in our Poetry. And . all this because the beautiful is not the product of our own fantasy, nor of our subjective perception, but has an objective existence, being itself the expression of a Divine perfection. After the Creation, God saw that all things were good. Imagine that every human eye were closed and every human ear stopped up, even then the beautiful remains, and God sees it and hears it, for, not only "His Eternal Power", but also His "Divinity", from the very creation, has been perceived in his creature, both spiritually and somatically. An artist may notice this in himself. If he realizes how his own art capacity depends upon his having an eye for art, he must necessarily come to the conclusion that the original eye for art is in God Himself, Whose art capacity is all-producing, and after Whose image the artist among men was made. We know this from the creation around us, from the firmament that overarches us, from the abounding luxury of nature, from the wealth of forms in man and animal, from the rushing sound of the stream and from the song of the nightingale; for how could all this beauty exist, except created by One Who preconceived the beautiful in His own Being, and produced it from His own Divine perfection? Thus you see that the

Sovereignty of God, and our creation after His Likeness, necessarily lead to that high interpretation of the
origin, the nature and the vocation of art, as adopted
by Calvin, and still approved by our own artistic instinct. The world of sounds, the world of forms, the
world of tints, and the world of poetic ideas, can have
no other source than God; and it is our privilege as
bearers of His image, to have a perception of this
beautiful world, artistically to reproduce, and humanly
to enjoy it.

And thus I come to my third and last point. We
found that the want of an art-style of its own, far
from being an objection to Calvinism, on the contrary
indicates the higher stage of its development. After
that, we considered how exalted an interpretation of
the nature of art flows from the Calvinistic principle.
And now let us see how nobly Calvinism has encouraged
the progress of the arts both in principle and in practice.
And here, in the first place, I draw your attention
to the important fact that it was Calvinism which, by
releasing art from the guardianship of the Curch, first
recognized its majority. I do not deny that the Renaissance had the same tendency, but, with the
Renaissance, this was marred by a too one-sided preference for the Paganistic, and a passion for ideas
more Heathen than Christian; while Calvin, on the
other hand, kept firmly to the Christian ideas, and more
sharply even than any other Reformer opposed every
Paganistic influence. To deal justly however with the older

Christian Church a somewhat fuller explanation is here
in place. The Christian Religion made its appearance
in the Greek and Roman world, which, though thoroughly demoralized, still recommended itself by its
high civilization and its artistic splendour. Therefore,
in order to oppose principle to principle, Christianity
was bound, at the outset, to react against the then-
dominating overestimation of art, and thereby to break
the dangerous influence which Paganism was exercising,
in its last convulsion, by the enchantment of its beautiful world. As long, therefore, as the struggle with
Paganism remained a struggle for life or death, the
relation of Christianity to art could not but be an
hostile one. This first period was followed almost immediately by the influx into the highly civilized Roman
Empire of the still almost barbaric Germanic tribes,
after whose speedy baptism the centre of power gradually removed from Italy to beyond the Northern
Alps, thus giving, to the Church, as early as the 8th
century an almost exclusive ascendency over the whole
of Europe. Thanks to this constellation, the Church
for several centuries became the guardian of higher
human life, and so nobly did she acquit herself of this
exalted task that no religious hatred or party prejudice
dares question any longer the glorious result she then
achieved. In the literal sense of the word, all human
development of that period depended entirely upon the
church. No science and no art could prosper unless
shielded by ecclesiastical protection. And hence originated that specifically Christian art, which, in its first
passion, tried to embody the maximum of spiritual

essence in the minimum of form and tint and tone. It was no art copied from nature, but art invoked from out the spheres of heaven, which fettered music in the Gregorian chains, the pencil and chisel of which longed after acosmic creations, and which only in the building of the cathedrals attained the really Sublime and reaped imperishable fame. All educational guardianship, meanwhile, leads to its own dissolution. A right-minded guardian intends to render his guardianship superfluous as soon as possible, and he who tries to prolong his control, even after his ward has reached maturity, creates an unnatural relation and makes his guardianship itself an incentive to resistance. When therefore the first education of Northern Europe was completed, and the church still persisted in swaying her absolute sceptre across the entire domain of life, four great movements were started from as many different sides, *viz.*, the *Renaissance*, in the domain of art, the *Republicanism* of Italy in politics, *Humanism* in science, and centrally, in Religion, the *Reformation*.

No doubt these four movements received their impulse from very different, and in some cases conflicting principles, but they all agreed on this one point, *viz.*, that they tried to escape from ecclesiastical tutelage, and to create a life of their own in accordance with their own principle. Hence it is not at all surprising, that, in the 16th century, these four powers repeatedly acted in concert. It was the one human life that, weary of any further guardianship, hastened in every way after a freer development, and therefore, when the old guardian tried by main force to hold back the declaration of maturity, it was but natural that those four powers should encourage one another fiercely to resist, nor to desist before freedom was obtained. Without this quadruple alliance not only would the tutelage of the church have persevered over all Europe, but — the rebellion once crushed — its rule would have become even more grievous and intolerable than beforehand. Thanks to this coöperation, the bold undertaking was crowned with enduring success, and the combatants, by their combined energy, earned the everlasting glory of having brought art and science, as well as politics and Religion, to the full enjoyment of maturity.

Will it be fair on this ground to assert that Calvinism has freed Religion, and not Art, and that the honours of the emancipation of art belong exclusively to the Renaissance? I readily grant that the Renaissance has a right to claim its share of the victory, especially in so far as it stimulated art herself to vindicate her liberty by her wonderful productions. Aesthetic genius, if I may so call it, had been implanted by God Himself in the Greek, and only by hailing again, amid loud rejoicings, the fundamental laws of art, which Greek genius had discovered, could art justify her claim to an independent existence. This by itself however could not have achieved the desired liberation. For the church of those days did not in the least oppose classical art as such. On the contrary, she welcomed the Renaissance, and Christian art did not hesitate a moment to enrich herself with the best the Renaissance had to offer. In the so-called *Cinquecento*, or high-Renaissance, Bramante and Da Vinci, Michael Angelo

and Raphael stored the Romish Cathedrals with treasures of art, quite unique and inimitable, never to be
surpassed. Thus the old tie continued to unite church
and art, and this of itself established a permanent
patronage. The real liberation of art required much
more patent energies. From principle, the church was
to be forced back to her spiritual realm. Art, having
hitherto confined herself to the holy spheres, had now
to make her appearance in the social world. And in
the church, Religion had to put aside her symbolical
robes, in order that, after having ascended to the higher
spiritual level, her life-giving breath might animate the
whole world. Just as Von Hartmann truly observes:
"It is pure spiritual Religion which with one hand de-
prives the artist of his specifically religious art, but
which, with the other, offers him, in exchange, a whole
world, to be religiously animated." Now Luther certainly
desired such a pure, spiritual Religion, but Calvinism was
the first to *grasp* it   First under the stirring impulses of
Calvinism, our fathers broke with the *splendor ecclesiae*,
i. e., with her outward glitter, and so also with her vast
possessions; by which art was financially held in bondage.
And although Humanism rebelled against this oppressive and unnatural state of things, it could never hope
to effect a radical change if left to its own resources.
Only think of Erasmus. Triumph in the struggle of
that time was not reserved for the man who carried
on the strife for Religious liberty by mere criticism,
but only for him, who, standing on an higher stage of
religious development, overcame the symbolical religion
as such. And, therefore, we may boldly assert that it

was Calvinism which prompted the spirited impulse by
which the victory was won, and, by its indefatigable
perseverance, has put an end to the unjustified tutelage
of the church over all human life, art included.

Meanwhile I readily grant that this outcome would
have been purely accidental, if Calvinism had not, at
the same time, led to a deeper interpretation of human
life and so of human art. When, under Victor Emmanuel,
with the help of Garibaldi, Italy was made free, the
day of liberty also dawned for the Waldenses, in Middle
and Southern Italy, but neither the *Re galantuomo*,
nor Garibaldi, had even thought of the Waldensians.
Thus it were possible that in its struggle for human
liberty Calvinism also cut the tie that thus far held art
a captive, but without having in the least intended to
do this, by virtue of its principle. And therefore I
must still illustrate the second factor, which alone decides the case. I have already, more than once, called
your attention to the important significance of the
Calvinistic doctrine of "common grace", and of course
in this lecture on art, I must refer to it again. That
which is to be ecclesiastical must bear the stamp of faith,
therefore genuine *Christian* art can only go out from believers. Calvinism, on the contrary, has taught us that all
liberal arts are gifts which God imparts promiscuously to
believers and to unbelievers, yea, that, as history shows,
these gifts have flourished even in a larger measure
outside the holy circle. "These radiations of Divine
Light," he wrote, "shone more brilliantly among unbelieving people than among God's saints." And this of
course quite reverses the proposed order of things. If

you limit the higher enjoyment of art to regeneration, then this gift is exclusively the portion of believers, and must bear an ecclesiastical character. In that case it is the outcome of *particular grace*. But if, at the hand of experience and history, you become persuaded that the highest art-instincts are *natural* gifts, and hence belong to those excellent graces which, in spite of sin, by virtue of *common grace*, have continued to shine in human nature, it plainly follows that art can inspire both believers *and* unbelievers, and that God remains Sovereign to impart it, in His good pleasure, alike to Heathen and to Christian nations. This applies not only to art, but to all the natural utterances of human life, and is illustrated by the comparison in early times between Israel and the other nations. As far as holy things are concerned, Israel is chosen, and is not only blessed above all nations, but stands among all nations, isolated. In the question of Religion, Israel has not only a larger share, but Israel *alone* has the truth, and all the other nations, even the Greeks and the Romans, are bent beneath the yoke of falsehood. Christ is not partly of Israel and partly of the nations; He is of Israel alone. Salvation is of the Jews. But just in proportion as Israel shines forth from within the domain of Religion, so is it equally backward when you compare the development of its art, science, politics, commerce and trade to that of the surrounding nations. The building of the Temple required the coming of Hiram from a heathen country to Jerusalem; and Solomon, in whom, after all, was found the Wisdom of God, not only knows that Israel stands

behind in architecture and needs help from without,
but by his action he publicly shows that he, as the
king of the Jews is in no way ashamed of Hiram's
coming, which he realizes as a natural ordinance of God.

So, Calvinism, on the ground both of the Scriptures
and of history, has arrived at the confession, that,
wherever the Sanctuary discloses itself, all unbelieving
nations stand outside, but that nevertheless, in their
secular history, they are called by God to a special
vocation, and form by their very existence, an indispensable link in the long chain of phenomena. Every
utterance of human life requires a special disposition in
blood and in descent, and proper adaptations of lot
and incident as well as of natural environment and
climatic effects are to contribute to its development.
In Israel all this was adapted to the holy heritage which
it was to receive in the Divine Revelation. But if Israel
was chosen for the sake of Religion, this in no way
prevented a parallel election of the Greeks for the
domain of philosophy and for the revelations of art,
nor of the Romans, for the classical development within
the domain of Law and of State. The life of art also
has both its provisional development, and its later un-
foldings, but in order to insure a more vigorous growth,
it wanted first of all clear self consciousness in its centrum that, once for all, the unchangeable foundations
of its ideal existence might be brought to light. Such
a phenomenon as art, arrives at this self-revelation once
only, and that revelation once granted to the Greek,
remains classical, tone-giving and for ever dominant.
And although a further art-development may seek

newer forms and richer material, the nature of the original find remains the same. Thus Calvinism was not only able, but bound, to confess that, by the grace of God, the Greeks were the primordial nation of art; that owing to this classical Greek development, art conquered its rights of independent existence; and that although it certainly ought to radiate also in the sphere of Religion, it should in no wise be engrafted in a dependent sense upon the ecclesiastical tree. Therefore, being a return of art to her rediscovered fundamental lines, the Renaissance did not present itself to Calvinism as a sinful effort, but as a divinely ordered movement. And as such Calvinism encouraged the Renaissance not by pure accident, but with clear consciousness and definite purpose, in accordance with its deepest principle.

Hence there is no question that, simply as an involuntary result of its opposition to the Hierarchy of Rome, Calvinism should at the same time have encouraged the emancipation of art. On the contrary, it demanded this liberation and was bound to effect it, within its own circle, as a consequence of its world- and life-view. The world after the fall is no lost planet, only destined now to afford the church a place in which to continue her combats; and humanity is no aimless mass of people which only serves the purpose of giving birth to the elect. On the contrary the world now, as well as in the beginning, is the theatre for the mighty works of God, and humanity remains a creation of His hand, which, apart from salvation, completes under this present dispensaton, here on earth, a mighty process, and in

its historical development is to glorify the name of
Almighty God. To this end He has ordained for this
humanity all sorts of life-utterances, and among these,
art occupies a quite independant place. Art reveals
ordinances of creation which neither science, nor politics,
nor religious life, nor even revelation can bring to
light. She is a plant that grows and blossoms upon her
own root, and without denying that this plant may
have required the help of a temporary support, and
that in early times the church lent this prop in a very
excellent way, yet the Calvinistic principle demanded
that this plant of earth should at length acquire strength
to stand alone and vigorously to extend its branches
in every direction. And thus Calvinism confessed that,
inasmuch as the Greeks had first discovered the laws
by which the growth of this art-plant is governed, they
therefore remain entitled to bind every further growth
and every new impulse of art to their first, their classical development. Not for the sake of stopping short
with Greece, or of adopting her Paganistic form without
criticism. Art, like Science, cannot afford to tarry at
her origin, but must ever develop herself more richly,
at the same time purging herself of whatsoever had
been falsely intermingled with the earlier plant. Only, the
law of her growth and life, when once discovered, must
remain the fundamental law of art for ever; a law, not
imposed upon her from without, but sprung from her
own nature. And so, by loosening every unnatural tie,
and cleaving to every tie that is natural, art must find the
inward strength required for the maintenance of her
liberty. Calvin therefore does not estrange art, science,

and religion, from one another; on the contrary, what
he desires is that all human life shall be permeated by
these three vital powers together. There must be a
Science which will not rest until it has thought out the
entire cosmos; a *Religion* which cannot sit still until
she has permeated every sphere of human life; and so
also there must be an *Art* which, despising no single
department of life adopts, into her splendid world, the
whole of human life, religion included.

Let this suggestion of the wide extension of the
domain of art introduce my last point, *viz.*, that
Calvinism has also *actually and in a concrete sense
advanced the development of the arts.* It scarcely
needs a reminder that, in the realm of art, Calvinism
was not able to play the role of a sorcerer, and
could only work with natural data. That the Italian
has a more tuneful voice than the Scot, and that the
German is carried away by a more passionate impulse
of song than the Netherlander, are simple data with
which art had to reckon, under Roman supremacy, as
well as under that of Calvinism. An undeniable fact,
which explains why it is neither logical nor honest to
reproach Calvinism for that which is merely due to
the differences of national character. The truth is
equally plain that, in the Northern countries of Europe,
Calvinism was not able to produce, as by magic, marble,
porphyry or free-stone, from the ground, and that
therefore the arts of sculpture and architecture, which
require rich, natural stone, were more readily developed

in those countries where quarries abound, than in a
country such as the Netherlands, where the ground
consists of clay and mire.   Poetry, music, and painting,
therefore, can alone be considered here, as the three
free arts that are most independent of all natural data.
This does not imply that the Flemish and Dutch city-
hall fails to hold a position of honor all its own among
the creations of architecture.   Louvain and Middleburg,
Antwerp and Amsterdam still bear witness to what
Dutch art wrought in stone.   And he who has seen
the statues in Antwerp and at the tomb of William
the Silent, carved by Quellinus and by De Keyzers,
does not question the ability of our artists of the chisel.
But this is subject to the objection that the style of
our City-Hall was found long before Calvinism made
its appearance in the Netherlands, and that, even in
its later development, it exhibits no single feature that
can remind one of Calvinism.   By virtue of its principle
Calvinism built no cathedrals, no palaces and no am-
phitheatres, and was unable to populate the vacant
niches of these gigantic buildings with sculptured or-
naments.

Indeed, the merits of Calvinism, with respect to art,
are to be found elsewhere.   Not in the objective, but
exclusively in the more subjective arts which, not de-
pending upon the patronage of wealth and not in want
of the marble quarry, have their spontaneous rise in
the human mind.   Of poetry I can make no further
mention, in this connection.   To that purpose I
should have to disclose to you the treasures of
our own Dutch Litterature, for the narrow bounds

within which our Netherland language is confined, have
excluded our poetry from the world at large. This
privilege of making their poetry a world phenomenon,
is only reserved for those larger nations, whose language,
being spoken by millions and millions, becomes a vehicle
for international intercourse. But if the province of
language for smaller nations is limited, the *eye* is international, and music heard by the *ear* is understood in
every heart. In order, therefore, that we may trace
the influence of Calvinism upon the development and
the welfare of art, we must limit ourselves, in the international sense, to the two subjective and independent
arts, those of *painting* and *music*.

Now of both these arts it is to be stated that, before
the days of Calvinism, they soared high above the common life of the Nations, and that only under the Calvinistic influence did they descend to the so much richer
life of the people. As regards painting, just recall the
productions of Dutch art by brush and etching-needle
in the 16th and 17th centuries. Rembrandt's name alone
is here sufficient to summon a whole world of art-
treasures before your mind's eye. The museums of every
country and continent still vie with each other, to the
utmost, in their efforts to obtain some specimen of his
work. Even your brokers have respect for an art-school
whose returns represent so vast a capital. And even in
our days the masters all over the world are still borrowing their most effectual motives and their best art-
tendencies from what, at that time, demanded the world's
admiration as an entirely new school of painting. Of
course this does not say that all these painters were

personally staunch Calvinists. In the earlier art-school,
which flourished under the influence of Rome the
"bon Catholiques" were also very rare. Such influences do not operate personally, but put their impress
upon surroundings and society, upon the world of
perceptions, of representations and of thought; and
as a result of these various impressions an art-school
makes its appearance. And, taken in this sense, the
antithesis between the past and the present in the
school of Dutch art is unmistakable. Before this period,
no account was taken of the people; *they* only were
considered worthy of notice who were superior to the
common man, *vis.*, the high world of the church and
of the priests, of knights and princes. But, since then,
the people had come of age, and under the auspices of
Calvinism, the art of painting, prophetic of a democratic
life of later times, was the first to proclaim the people's
maturity. The family ceased to be an annex to the
church, and asserted its standing in its independent
significance. By the light of common grace it was seen
that the non-churchly life was also possessed of high
importance and of an all-sided art-motive. Having
been overshadowed for many centuries by class-distinc-
tions, the common life of man came out of its hiding-
place like a new world, in all its sober reality. It was
the broad emancipation of our ordinary earthly life,
and the instinct for liberty, which thereby captured the
heart of the nations and inspired them with delight in
the enjoyment of treasures so long blindly neglected.
Even Taine has sounded the praises of the blessing,
which went forth from the Calvinistic love of liberty

to the realm of art, and Carrière, who himself was
equally far from sympathizing with Calvinism, loudly
proclaims that Calvinism alone was able to plough the
field on which free art could flourish.

It has frequently been remarked, moreover, that the
idea of election by free grace has contributed not a
little toward interesting art in the hidden importance
of what was seemingly small and insignificant. If a
common man, to whom the world pays no special attention, is valued and even chosen by God as one of
His elect, this must lead the artist also to find a motive
for his artistic studies in what is common and of every-
day occurrence, to pay attention to the emotions and
the issues of the human heart in it, to grasp with his
artistic instinct, their ideal impulse, and, lastly, by his
pencil to interpret for the world at large the precious
discovery he has made. Even foolish and drastic ex-
travagances became the motive for art-productions,
merely as revolutions, of the human heart and as
manifestations of human life. Man was also to be
shown the image of his folly, that he might depart
from evil. Thus far the artist had only traced upon
his canvass the idealized figures of prophets and apostles,
of saints and priests; now however, when he saw how
God had chosen the porter and the wage-earner for
Himself, he found interest not only in the head, the
figure and the entire personality of the man of the
people, but began to reproduce the human expression
of every rank and station. And if thus far the eyes
of all had been fixed constantly and solely upon the
sufferings of the "Man of Sorrows", some now began

15

to understand, that there was a mystical suffering also in the general woe of man, revealing hitherto unmeasured depths of the human heart, and thereby enabling us to fathom much better the still deeper depths of the mysterious agonies of Golgotha. Ecclesiastical power no longer restrained the artist, and princely gold no longer chained him in its fetters. If artist, he also was man, mingling freely among the people, and discovering in and behind their human life, something quite different from what palace and castle had hitherto afforded him, something, too, which proved to be much more valuable than the keenest eye had ever surmised. As Taine so significantly says: To Rembrandt, human life hid its face behind many sombre hues, but even in that chiaroscuro his grasp upon that life was profoundly real and significant. As the result therefore of the declaration of the people's maturity and of the love of liberty which Calvinism awakened in the heart of the nations, the commun but rich human life disclosed to art an entirely new world, and, by opening the eye for the small and the insignificant, and by opening the heart for the sorrows of mankind, from the rich content of this newly discovered world, the Dutch school of art has produced upon the canvass those wondrous art-productions which still immortalize its fame, and which have shown the way to all the nations for new conquests.

Finally, as to the significance Calvinism had for Music, we face one of its excellencies which, though less widely known, is notwithstanding highly important — as Mr. Douen taught us, ten years ago, in his two big volumes on Marot. Music and painting here run parallel.

Even as in the ecclesiastical-aristocratic period it was
only the high and the holy that interested the masters
of the pencil, so in music the plain chant of Gregory
was dominant, which abandoned rhythm, despised harmony, and which according to a professional critic, by
its provisionally conservative character barred the way
to the further artistic development of music. Far below
the level of this stately chant flowed the freer song of
the people, too often, alas, inspired by the worship of
Venus, which at the times of the so called "donkey-
festivals", much to the chagrin of ecclesiastical officials,
penetrated even the walls of the churches, and there
occasioned those repulsive scenes which the Council of
Trent first succeeded in putting under the ban. The
church alone was privileged to make music, while that
which the people produced was scorned, as being beneath the dignity of the art. Even in the oratory itself,
while the people were allowed to listen to the holy music,
they were forbidden to join in the song. Thus, as an
art, music was almost entirely deprived of its independent
standing. Only in so far as it could serve the church
was it permitted to flourish artistically. Whatever it
undertook on its own responsibility, had no higher call
than the popular use. And as in every department of
life, Protestantism in general, but Calvinism more consistently, bridled the tutelage of the church, so also was
music emancipated by it, and the way opened to its so
splendid modern development. The men who first
arranged the music of the Psalm for the Calvinistic
singing were the brave heroes who cut the strands
that bound us to the Cantus firmus, and selected their

melodies from the free world of music. To be sure,
by doing this, they adopted the people's melodies,
but as Douen rightly remarks, only in order that they
might return these melodies to the people purified and
baptized in Christian seriousness. Music also would
flourish, henceforth, not within the narrow limitations
of particular grace, but in the wide and fertile fields of
common grace. The choir was abandoned; in the
sanctuary the people themselves would sing, and therefore Bourgeois and the Calvinistic virtuosi who followed
him, were bound to make their selections from the
popular melodies, but with this end in view, *viz.*, that
now the people would no longer sing in the saloon or
in the street, but in the sanctuary, and thus, in their
melodies, cause the seriousness of the heart to triumph
over the heat of the lower passions.

If this is the general merit of Calvinism, or rather
the change which it effected in the domain of music,
by forcing the idea of the laity to give room to that
of the general priesthood of believers, historic accuracy
requires a still more concrete elucidation. If Bourgeois
was the great master whose works still assure him
a front rank among the most notable composers of
Protestant Europe, it is also worthy of note that this
Bourgeois lived and laboured in Geneva, under the very
eyes of Calvin and even partly under his direction. It
was this same Bourgeois who had the courage to adopt
rhythm and to exchange the eight Gregorian modes
for the two of major and minor from the popular music;
to sanctify its art in consecrated hymn, and so to put
the impress of honour upon that musical arrangement

of tunes, from which all modern music had its rise. In the same way Bourgeois adopted the harmony or the song of several parts. He was the man who wedded melody to verse by what is called *expression*. The solfeggio, *i.e.* the singing by note, the reduction of the number of chords, the clearer distinction of the several gamuts, etc., by which the knowledge of music was so much simplified, is all owing to the perseverance of this Calvinistic Composer. And when Goudimel, his Calvinistic colleague, once at Rome the teacher of the great Palestrine, listening to the singing of the people in the church, discovered that the higher voices of the children outstripped the tenor, which had thus far held the lead, he for the first time gave the leading part to the soprano; a change of far-reaching influence which has ever since been maintained.

Pardon me if for a moment I detained you with these particulars, but the merits of Protestantism, and more particularly of Calvinism, in music are of too high an order to suffer longer depreciation without protest. I fully acknowledge that Calvinism exercised over some arts only an indirect influence, by the declaration of their maturity, and by affording them liberty to flourish in their own independence, but on music, the influence of Calvinism was a very positive one, due to its spiritual worship of God, which provided no room for the more material arts, but assigned a new role to song and to music by the creation of melodies and songs for the people. Whatever the old school did to join itself to the newer development of music, the modern music remained unnatural to the cantus firmus,

because it sprang from a quite different root. Calvinism
on the other hand not only joined itself to it, but under
the leadership of Bourgeois and Goudimel gave it its
first impulse, so that even Roman Catholic writers are
constrained to acknowledge, that our beautiful development of music in the last and present centuries for the
most part owed its rise to the heretical church-hymns.

That in a later period Calvinism lost almost all influence in this domain, cannot be denied. For a long
time Anabaptism overwhelmed us with its dualistic
prejudices, and an unhealthy spiritualism prevailed.
But when on that account, with entire disregard of our
great musical past, Calvinism is accused by Rome of
aesthetic dullness, it is well to call to mind that the
great Goudimel was murdered by Romish fanaticism in
the massacre of St. Bartholomew. This fact is sug-
gestive; for we naturally ask with Douet, Has that
man any right to complain about the stillness of the
forest, who with his own hand has caught and killed
the nightingale.

CALVINISM AND THE FUTURE.

The chief purpose of my lecturing in this country was, to eradicate the wrong idea, that Calvinism represented an exclusively dogmatical and ecclesiastical movement.

Calvinism *did* not stop at a church-order, but expanded in a *life-system*, and did not exhaust its energy in a dogmatical construction, but created a *life* and *world-view*, and such a one as was, and still is, able to fit itself to the needs of every stage of human development, in every department of life. It raised our Christian religion to its highest spiritual splendour; it created a church order, which became the preformation of state confederation; it proved to be the guardian angel of science; it emancipated art; it propagated a political scheme, which gave birth to constitutional government, both in Europe and America; it fostered agriculture and industry, commerce and navigation; it put a thorough Christian Stamp upon home-life and family-ties; it promoted through its high moral standard

purety in our social circles; and to this manifold effect
it placed beneath Church and State, beneath society
and home-circle a fundamental philosophic conception,
strictly derived from its dominating principle, and
therefore all its own.

This of itself excludes every idea of imitative repristination, and what the descendants of the old Dutch
Calvinists as well as of the Pilgrim fathers have to do,
is not to copy the past, as if Calvinism were a petre-
fact, but to go back to the living root of the Calvinist
plant, to clean and to water it, and so to cause it to
bud and to blossom once more, now fully in accordance
with our actual life in these modern times. and with
the demands of the times to come.

This explains the subject of my final lecture. *A new
Calvinistic development needed by the wants of the future.*

The prospect of this future does not present itself to us,
as every student of sociology will acknowledge, in bright
colours. I would not go so far as to assert that we are on
the eve of universal social bankruptcy, but that the signs
of the times are ominous admits of no denial. To be
sure, in the control of nature and her forces, immense
gains are being registered year by year, and the boldest
imagination is unable to foretell to what heights of
power in this respect the race may attain in the next
half century. As a result of this, the comforts of life
are increasing. World-intercourse and communication
are constantly becoming more rapid and widespread.
Asia and Africa, until recently dormant, gradually feel
themselves drawn into the larger circle of stirring life.
Aided by sport, the principles of hygiene exert a grow-

ing influence. Consequently, we are physically stronger than the preceding generation. We live longer. And in combating the defects and infirmities that threaten and afflict our bodily life, surgical science makes us marvel at her achievements. In brief, the material, tangible side of life holds out the fairest of promises for the future.

And yet discontent makes itself heard, and the thinking mind cannot suppress its misgivings; for, however high one may value the material things, they do not fill out the round of our existence as men. Our personal life as men and citizens subsists not in the comforts that surround us, nor in the body, which serves us as a link with the outward world, but in the spirit that internally actuates us; and in this inner consciousness we are becoming more and more painfully aware, how the hypertrophy of our external life results in a serious atrophy of the spiritual. Not as if the faculties of thought and reflection, the arts of poetry and letters, were in abeyance. On the contrary, empirical science is more brilliant in her attainments than ever, universal knowledge spreads in constantly widening circles, and civilization, in Japan, for instance, is almost dazzled by her too-rapid conquests. But even the intellect does not constitute the mind. Personality is seated more deeply in the hidden recesses of our inner being, where character is formed, whence the flame of enthusiasm is kindled, where the moral foundations are laid, where love's blossoms bud, whence spring consecration and heroism, and where in the sense for the Infinite, our time-bound existence reaches out

unto the very gates of eternity. It is in regard to this
seat of personality that we hear on all sides the complaint of empoverishment, degeneracy and petrifaction.
The prevalence of this state of *malaise* explains the
rise of a spirit like Arthur Schopenhauer's; and the
wide acceptance of his pessimistic doctrine reveals to
what a deplorable extent this fatal Sirocco has scorched
already the fields of life. It is true, Tolstoi's efforts
show force of character, but even his religious and
social theory is a protest along the whole line against
the spiritual degeneracy of our race. Friedrich Wilhelm,
Nietzsche may give us offence by his sacrilegious mockery,
still what else is his demand for the "*Uebermensch*"
(over-man), but the cry of despair wrung from the heart
of humanity by the bitter consciousness that it is spiritually pining away. What is Social-democracy also but
one gigantic protest against the insufficiency of the
existing order of things. Even Anarchism and Nihilism
but too plainly demonstrate that there are thousands
upon ten thousands who would rather demolish and
annihilate everything, than continue to bear the burden
of present conditions. The German author of the
"*Decadenz der Völker*" descries nothing in the future
but decay and social ruin. Even the sober-minded Lord
Salisbury recently spoke of peoples and states for whose
unceremonious burial preparations were already being
made. How often has not the parallel been drawn between
our time and the golden age of the Roman empire, when
the external brilliancy of life likewise dazzled the eye,
notwithstanding that the social diagnosis could yield no
other verdict than "rotten to the very core". And,

although on the American continent, in a younger
world, a relatively healthier tone of life prevails than in
senescent Europe, yet this will not for a moment mis-
lead the thinking mind. It is impossible for you to
shut yourselves off hermetically from the old world, as
you form no humanity apart, but are a member of the
great body of the race. And the poison having once
entered the system at a single point in due time must
necessarily pervade the whole organism.

Now the serious question with which we are confronted is whether we can expect that by natural evolution a higher phase of social life will develop out of
the present spiritual decline. The answer history supplies
to this question is far from encouraging. In India, in
Babylon, in Egypt, in Persia, in China and elsewhere,
like periods of vigorous growth have been succeeded
by times of spiritual decadence; and yet in not one of
these lands has the downward course finally resolved
itself in a movement towards higher things. All these
nations to this day have persevered in their spiritual
stagnation. In the Roman empire alone has the dark
night of boundless demoralisation been broken by the
dawn of a higher life. But this light did not arise
through evolution; it shone from the Cross of Calvary.
The Christ of God had appeared, and by his Gospel
alone was the society of that time saved from certain
destruction. And again, when towards the close of
the middle ages Europe was threatened with social
bankruptcy, a second resurrection from the dead and

a manifestation of new vital power were witnessed, now among the peoples of the Reformation, but this time also not by way of evolution, but again through the same Gospel for which the hearts were thirsting and whose truth was freely proclaimed as never before. What antecedents then does history furnish to lead us to expect in the present instance an evolution of life from death, whilst the symptoms of decomposition already suggest the bitterness of the grave? Mohammed, it is true, in the seventh century succeeded in creating a stir among the dead bones throughout the entire Levant by throwing himself upon the nations as a second Messiah, greater even than the Christ. And assuredly if the coming of another Christ, surpassing in glory the Christ of Bethlehem, were possible, then the cure for moral corruption were found. Hence some indeed have been anxiously looking for the coming of some glorious "Universal Spirit", who might again instil his vitalizing power into the heart-blood of the nations. But why dwell longer on such idle fancies? Nothing *can* possibly surpass the God-given Christ, and what we are to look for, instead of a second Messiah, is the second coming of the same Christ of Calvary, this time with His fan in His hand for judgment, not to open up for our sin-cursed life a new evolution, but to receive at its goal and solemnly to conclude the history of the world. Either this second coming, therefore, is near at hand, and what we are witnessing are the death-throes of humanity; or a rejuvenation is still in store for us; but if so, that rejuvenation can come only through the old and yet ever new Gospel which at the beginning of our era, and again at the time of the Reformation, has saved the threatened life of our race.

The most alarming feature, however, of the present situation is the lamentable absence of that receptivity in our diseased organism, which is indispensable to the effecting of a cure. In the Graeco-Roman world such receptivity did exist; the hearts opened spontaneously to receive the truth. To an even stronger degree this receptivity existed in the age of the Reformation, when large masses cried for the gospel. Then as now the body suffered from anæmia, and blood-poisning even had set in, but there was no aversion to the only effectual antidote. Now it is precisely this that distinguishes our modern decadence from the two preceding ones, that with the masses the receptivity for the Gospel in on the decrease, whilst with the scientists the positive aversion to it is on the increase. The invitation to bow the knee before Christ, as God, is met so often with a shrug of the shoulders, if not with the sarcastic rejoinder: "Fit for children and old women, not for us men!" The modern philosophy, which gains the day, considers itself in ever increasing measure as having *outgrown* Christianity.

Therefore, first of all, the question must be answered what has brought us to this pass, a question deriving its paramount importance from the fact that only a correct diagnosis can lead to effective treatment. Now, historically, the cause of the evil is found in nothing else than in the spiritual degeneration which marked the close of the preceding century. The reponsibility for this degeneration undoubtedly rests in part with the Christian churches themselves, not excepting those of the Reformation. Worn out by their struggle with Rome, these last churches had fallen asleep, had allowed leaf and flower to wither on their branches, and had apparently become forgetful of their duties in reference to humanity at large and the whole sphere of human life. It is not necessary to enter upon this more fully. It may be taken for granted that towards the end of that century the general tone of life had become vapid and common-place, ignoble and base at heart. The eagerly devoured literature of the period furnishes the proof. By way of reaction against this, the proposal was then made by deistic and atheistic philosophers, first in England, but afterwards chiefly in France on the part of the Encyclopaedists, to place the whole of life on a new basis, turn upside down the existing order of affairs, and arrange a new world on the assumption that human nature continues in its incorrupted state. This conception was an heroic one and awakened response; it struck some of the noblest chords of the human heart. But in the great Revolution of 1789 it was put into execution in its most dangerous form; for in this mighty revolution, in this upheaval not only of political conditions, but even more of convictions, ideas, and usages of life, two elements should be sharply distinguished. In one respect it was an imitation of Calvinism, whilst in another respect it was in direct opposition to its principles. The great Revolution, it should not be forgotten, broke out in a

Roman-Catholic country, where first in the night of St. Bartholomew and subsequently by the revocation of the edict of Nantes, the Huguenots had been slaughtered and banished. After this violent suppression of Protestantism in France, and other Roman-Catholic countries, the ancient despotism had regained its ascendency, and to these nations all the fruits of the Reformation had been lost. This, by way of caricature of Calvinism, invited and compelled the attempt to strike for freedom by external violence and to establish a pseudo-democratic state of affairs, which was to preclude for ever a return to despotism. Thus the French revolution, by meeting violence with violence, crime with crime, strove after the same social liberty which Calvinism had proclaimed among the nations, but which had been attempted by Calvinism in the course of a purely spiritual movement. By this the French revolution in a sense executed a judgment of God, the result of which affords, even to Calvinists, cause for rejoicing. The shades of De Coligny were avenged in the September-murders of Mazas.

But this is only one side of the medal. Its reverse discloses a purpose directly *opposed* to the sound Calvinistic idea of liberty. Calvinism by virtue of its profoundly serious conception of life had strengthened and consecrated the social and ethical ties; the French revolution loosened and entirely unfastened them, detaching life not merely from the Church but also from God's ordinances, even from God Himself. Man as such, each individual henceforth, was to be his own lord and master, guided by his own free will and good pleasure. The train

of life was to rush forward even more rapidly then
heretofore, but no longer bound to follow the track of
the divine commandments. What else could result than
wreckage and ruin? Enquire of the France of to-day
what fruit the fundamental idea of her grand Revolution
has yielded to the nation after its first century of free
sway so rich in horrors, and the answer comes in a
most pitiful tale of national decadence and social demoralisation.

Humbled by the enemy from beyond the Rhine,
internally rent by partisan fury, dishonoured by the
Panama cabal, and more still by the Dreyfus-case,
disgraced by its pornography, the victim of œconomic
retrogression, stationary, nay, even decreasing in population, France, as has been well said by Dr. Garnier,
a medical authority on the subject, France has been
led by egotism to degrade mariage, by lust to destroy
family-life, and presents to-day, in wide circles, the
disgusting spectacle of men and women lost in unnatural
sexual sin 1). I am aware that there are still thousands
upon thousands of families in France living without

---

1) Dr. GARNIER, l'Onanisme, Paris 1893. p. 31: La philosophie du
dix-huitième siècle ramena l'épidémie érotique du moyen âge. Vivement
préoccupés des choses de l'amour physique, ce qui était le reflet et l'expression de mœurs aussi dépravées qu'à aucune autre époque, tous les
écrivains les traduisirent avec une hardiesse de pensée, une liberté de
langage sous les formes les plus variées. La corruption s'empara de toutes
les classes de la société, sans être aussi impétueuse et originale qu'au
moyen âge et dans l'antiquité. Le tempérament n'était plus le même.
Moins grandiose et monstrueuse, la débauche était plus raisonnée et phi-
losophique. Dans ce siècle de l'Encyclopédie et de la vulgarisation, le
vice ne se donnait plus la peine de se cacher; au contraire, il s'étalait au
grand jour, comme pour se venger des réticences hypocrites et forcées que

reproach, who dearly grieve at the moral ruin of their
country, but then these are the very circles which have
resisted the false pretences of the Revolution; and, on
the other hand, the almost bestialized circles are those,
that have succumbed to the first onset of Voltairianism.

From France this spirit of dissolution, this passion of
wild emancipation, has spread among the other nations,
especially through the medium of an infamously obscene

la fin du siècle de Louis XIV lui avait imposées. Il semblait vouloir
s'expliquer et se justifier pour faire école.

De là l'éclosion de cette littérature immonde, décrivant tous les désor-
dres et les aberrations des sens et les enseignant avec un mélange de
frénésie et de méthode rationnelle, dont il n'y avait pas encore eu d'exemple.
Une sorte de pédantisme cynique, dont les plus grands écrivains offrent
une teinte plus ou moins prononcée, en est la caractéristique. Ces étranges
obscénités étaient écrites en français, comme la langue la plus répandue
et qui s'y prêtait le mieux. Débités presque ouvertement en France, ces
écrits inondèrent l'Europe et le monde, bien qu'il n'en reste plus guère
que de rares exemplaires. Sortis de la corruption, ils la formulèrent sous
tous ses modes, même les plus abjects, et ils la propagèrent avec toute
la fougue du prosélytisme, dit le docteur Mauriac.

Des ouvrages de médecine furent composés à cette époque pour réagir
contre ces excès et combattre les abus érotiques, l'onanisme en particulier.
Ce n'est pas que ce vice fût plus commun ni dangereux qu'antérieurement;
le public seul prenait goût à ces lectures et trouvait dans ces détails
techniques sur les organes sexuels, leurs fonctions et leurs maladies, un
nouvel aliment pour satisfaire sa curiosité. De là leur vogue, leur succès
augmentant depuis avec les dépravations dont ils traitent, et les maladies,
les infirmités qui en sont la conséquence, comme l'abaissement de la
natalité en France en est aujourd'hui la plus grande calamité.

Suivant la tradition du dix-huitième siècle, l'onanisme, sous-entendant
la masturbation seule, était considéré comme le plus grand fléau de l'humanité, d'après l'opinion exprimée dans les ouvrages publiés à cette époque.
Cette opinion fit leur succès. A moins d'un siècle d'intervalle, elle a
complètement changé. C'est tout le contraire actuellement avec le positi-

16

literature, and infected their lives.   Then nobler minds particularly in Germany, perceiving what depth of wickedness had been reached in France, made the bold attempt of realizing this enticing and reducing idea of "emancipation from God" in a higher form while yet retraining its essence.   Philosophers of the first rank in a stately procession each for himself constructed a cosmology endeavoring to restore a firm foundation

visme régnant et le matérialisme en vogue. On ne considère plus ces monstruosités immorales, ces affreuses turpitudes, que comme remplaçant ou suppléant l'acte physiologique en cas de besoin, sinon comme des perversions, des aberrations morbides de la fonction génésique. On ne les incrimine plus et l'on invoque même l'hygiène, la santé et la maladie pour les justifier, les légitimer par des exemples et des observations concluantes. „Sachons le reconnaître, dit le docteur Christian, l'onanisme est une de ces maladies morales avec lesquelles l'humanité est obligée de vivre. „Loin d'en atténuer la fréquence, il proclame que nul n'échappe entièrement à son action. On ne l'avoue guère cependant que dans l'enfance, l'inconscience supposée de cet acte lui servant d'excuse.

Ainsi se trouve envisagée la question dans le plus récent dictionnaire de médecine en cours de publication, chargé d'exprimer l'état actuel de la science. On veut par là le réduire à sa plus simple expression. Les philosophes et les moralistes positivistes, s'inspirant de ces données pour tirer la morale de ces vices contre nature, n'auront plus qu'à les approuver et les absoudre. De là l'assentiment et l'accommodation générale à ces pratiques honteuses, qui forment la plaie actuelle de la société française en particulier.

Aussi bien, son état apparent est-il en parfaite conformité avec ces doctrines. Le relâchement des mœurs est ainsi rendu public par l'augmentation des unions bâtardes, le pseudo-célibat des deux sexes et l'illégitimité. On ne se marie plus, sinon exceptionnellement, parmi les nombreuses populations livrées au commerce et à l'industrie, que par calcul, comme dans la bourgeoisie. De là le retard des unions légitimes, dont le peu de cohésion ou la dissolution s'accuse ostensiblement par la progression des séparations, des divorces et la diminution croissante de la natalité en France.

to social and ethical relations, either by putting them
on the basis of natural law, or by giving them an
ideal substratum evolved from their own speculation.
For a moment this attempt seemed to have a fair
chance of success; for, instead of atheistically banish-
ing God from their system, these philosophers sought
refuge in Pantheism, and thus made it feasible to found
the social structure, not as the French, on a state of
nature or on the atomistic will of the individual, but
on the processes of history and the collective will of
the race, unconsciously tending towards the highest
goal. And, indeed, for more than half a century this
philosophy has imparted a certain stability to life; not
that any real stability was inherent in the systems
themselves, but because the established order of law
and strong political institutions in Germany lent the
indirect support of tradition to the walls of an edifice
which otherwise would have immediately collapsed.
Even so, however, it could not prevent that in Germany, also, moral principles became more and more
problematic, moral foundations more and more insecure,
no other right than that of actual law received recognition; and, however much German and French development might differ between themselves, both agreed
in their aversion to, and rejection of, traditional Christianity. Voltaire's *"Ecrasez l'infâme"* is already left
far behind by Nietzsche's blasphemous utterances on
the Christ, and Nietzsche is the author whose works
are being most eagerly devoured by the young *modern*
Germany of our day.

After this manner then, we in Europe at least, have

arrived at what is callad *modern life*, involving a radical
breach with the Christian traditions of the Europe of the
past.   The spirit of this *modern life* is   most clearly
marked by the fact that it seeks the origin of man not in
creation after the image of God but in evolution from the
animal.   Two fundamental ideas are clearly implied in this:
1. that the point of depature is no longer the ideal or
the divine, but the material and the low; 2. that the
sovereignty of God, which ought to be supreme, is
denied, and man yields himself to the mystical current
of an endless process, a *regressus* and *processus in in-
finitum*.   Out of the root of these two fertile ideas a
double type of life is now being evolved.   On the one
hand the interesting, rich, and highly-organized life of
University-circles, attainable by the more refined minds
only; and at the side of this, or rather far beneath it,
a materialistic life of the masses, craving after pleasure,
but, in their own way, also taking their point of departure in matter, and likewise, but after their own cynical
fashion, emancipating themselves from all fixed ordinances.   Especially in our ever-expanding large cities
this second type of life is gaining the upper hand, and,
overriding the voice of the country-districts, and is giving
a shape to public opinion, which avows its ungodly
character more openly in each successive generation.
Money, pleasure and social power, these alone are the
objects of pursuit; and people are constantly growing
less fastidious regarding the means employed to secure
them.   Thus the voice of conscience becomes less and
less audible, and duller the lustre of the eye which on
the eve of the French revolution still reflected some

gleam of the ideal. The fire of all higher enthusiasm
has been quenched, only the dead embers remain. In
the midst of the weariness of life, what can restrain
the disappointed from taking refuge in suicide? Deprived
of the wholesome influence of rest, the brain is over-
stimulated and over-exerted till the asylums are no longer
adequate for housing the insane. Whether property be
not synonymous with theft, becomes a more and more
seriously mooted question. That life ought to be freer
and marriage less binding, is being accepted more and
more on an established proposition. The cause of
monogamy is no longer worth fighting for, since poly-
gamy and polyandry are being systematically glorified
in all products of the realistic school of art and literature. In harmony with this, religion is of course
declared superfluous because it renders life gloomy.
But art, art above all, is in demand, not for the sake
of its ideal worth, but because it pleases and intoxi-
cates the senses. Thus people live in time and for
temporal things, and shut their ears to the tolling of
the bells of eternity. The irrepressible tendency is to
make the whole view of life concrete, concentrated,
practical. And out of this modernized private life there
emerges a type of social and political life characterized
by a decadence of parliamentarism, by an ever stronger
desire for a dictator, by a sharp conflict between pau-
perism and capitalism, whilst heavy armaments on land
and on sea, even at the price of financial ruin, become the
ideal of these powerful states whose craving for territorial
expansion threatens the very existence of the weaker
nations. Gradually the conflict between the strong and

the weak has grown to be the controlling feature of
life, arising from Darwinism itself, whose central idea
of a *struggle for life* has for its mainspring this very
antithesis. Since Bismarck introduced it into higher
politics, the maxim of the right of the stronger has
found almost universal acceptance. The scholars and
experts of our day demand with increasing boldness
that the common man shall bow to their authority.
And the end can only be that once more the sound
principles of democracy will be banished, to make room
this time not for a new aristocracy of nobler birth and
higher ideals, but for the coarse and overbearing *kra-
tistocracy* of a brutal money-power. Nietzsche is by
no means exceptional, but proclaims as its herald the
future of our modern life. And while the Christ in
divine compassion showed heart-winning sympathy with
the weak, modern life in this respect also takes the
precisely opposite ground that the weak must be supplanted by the strong. Such, they tell us, *was* the
process of selection to which we, ourselves, owe our
origin, and such is the process which, in us and after
us, must work itself out to its ultimate consequences.

Meanwhile, as observed above, it should not be forgotten that there flows in modern life a side-current,
of nobler oringin. A host of high-minded men arose,
who, shrinking from the uneasy chill of the moral
atmosphere, and taking alarm at the brutality of the
previling egotism, endeavored to strengthen the low-
ebbing life partly by means of altruism, partly by

means of a mystical cult of the feelings, partly even by means of the name of Christianity. Though in accord with the school of the French Revolution in their breach with Christian tradition and in their refusal to recognize any point of departure besides that of empiricism and rationalism, these men nevertheless, by acquiescing, as Kant in a gross dualism, tried to escape from the fatal consequences of their principle. It is precisely from this dualism that they drew the inspiration for the many noble ideas elaborated in their theories, embodied in their poetry, conjured up before our imagination in touching romances, commended to our consciences in ethical treatises, and, best of all, realized not unfrequently in the serious pursuit of life. With them side with the intellect, conscience had maintained its authority, for, even where God is forsaken, conscience, being divinely touched, remains capable of producing, to a certain extent, pure and sound emotions. To the vigorous initiative of these men we owe the numerous Sociological investigations and practical measures, which have allayed and alleviated so much suffering, and by an ideal altruism have put to shame the selfishness even of so many a Christian heart. Having a personal predisposition for mysticism, some of them claimed the right to emancipate the inner life of the soul from all restraints of criticism. To lose one's self in the Infinite, and to feel the stream of the Infinite pulsate through the deepest recesses of the inner life, meant to them the highest raptures of piety.—Others again—specially theologians,—to a less extent divorced from Christianity by reason of their antecedents, office

or scholarly occupation, falling in with this altruism
and mysticism, set themselves the task of so
metamorphosing the Christ that he might continue to
glitter from the throne of humanity, as the highest
ideal of the modernized human heart. Each and all
inspired by sincerity and inspiring by their ideal intent,
these endeavours may be traced from Schleiermacher
down to Ritschl. He, therefore, who would look down,
upon such men would only dishonour himself. Much
rather we ought to thank them for what they endeavored to save, also those women of noble aspirations,
who by their character-novels, written in an elevated
Christian spirit, have counteracted so much that was
base, and have fostered so many precious germs. Even
Spiritism, fraught with errour though it be, has often
received its impulse from the alluring hope that the
contact with the eternal world, destroyed by criticism,
could thus be reëstablished through the medium of
visions. Unfortunately, however boldly conceived this
ethical dualism might be, and whatever bold metamorphoses this mysticism might indulge in, there always
lurked behind it the naturalistic, rationalistic system of
thought which the intellect had devised. They extolled
the normal character of their cosmology over against
the abnormalism of our belief; and the Christian religion, being abnormalistic in principle and its mode of
manifestation, inevitably lost ground, to such an extent
that some of our best men did not shrink from pro-
fessing that they preferred not only Spiritism but
Mohammedanism, and Schopenhauer even Buddhism to
the old Evangelical Faith. It is true that the entire

phalanx of theologians from Schleiermacher to Pfleiderer continued to pay high honours to the name of Christ, but it is equally undeniable that this remained possible only by subjecting Christ and the Christian confession to ever bolder metamorphoses. A painful fact, but one which becomes absolutely evident, if you compare the creed now current in these circles with the confession for which our Martyrs died.

Even confining ourselves to the Apostles' creed, which for almost two a thousand years substantially has been the Common standard of all Christians, we find that the belief in God as the "Creator of heaven and earth" has been abolished; for creation has been supplanted by evolution. Abolished also has been the belief in God the Son, as born of the Virgin Mary, through conception from the Holy Ghost. Abolished further, with many, the belief in His resurrection and ascension and return to judgment. Abolished finally even the belief of the church in the resurrection of the dead, or at least in the resurrection of the body. The name of the Christian religion is still being retained, but in essence it has become a quite different religion in its principle, even of a diametrically opposite character. And when incessantly the charge is brought against us, that in point of fact the traditional Christ of the Church involves a complete metamorphosis of the genuine Jesus, whilst the modern interpretation has lifted the veil off the true character of the historical Jesus of Nazareth, we can but answer, that after all, historically, not this modern conception of Jesus of Nazareth but the Church's confession of the God-Man

is the one that has conquered the world; and that
throughout those fifty ages the best and most pious of
our race have paid homage to the Christ of tradition
and rejoiced in Him as their Saviour in the shadow of
Death.

Though desiring to be second to none, therefore, in
sincere appreciation of what is noble in such attempts,
I am fully settled in my conviction that no help is
to be expected from that quarter. A theology which
virtually destroys the authority of the Holy Scriptures
as a sacred book; which sees in sin nothing but a
lack of development; recognises Christ for no more
than a religious genius of central significance; views
redemption as a mere reversal of our subjective mode
of thinking; and indulges in a mysticism dualistically
opposed to the world of the intellect,—such a theology
is like a dam giving way before the first assault of the
inrushing tide. It is a theology without hold upon the
masses, a quasi-religion utterly powerless to restore our
sadly tottering moral life to even a temporary footing.

May more perhaps be expected from the marvellous
energy displayed in the latter half of this century by
Rome? Let us not too hastily dismiss this question.
Though the history of the Reformation has etablished
a fundamental antithesis between Rome and ourselves,
it would nevertheless be narrow-minded and short-sighted
to underestimate the real power which even now is
manifest in Rome's warfare against Atheism and Pantheism. Only ignorance of the exhaustive studies of

Romish philosophy and of Rome's successful efforts in
social life, could account for such a superficial judgment.
Calvin in his day already acknowledged that, as against
a spirit from the Great Deep, he considered Romish
believers his allies. A so-called orthodox Protestant
need only mark in his confession and catechism such
doctrines of religion and morals as are not subject to
controversy between Rome and ourselves, to perceive
immediately, that what we have in common with Rome
concerns precisely those fundamentals of our Christian
creed now most fiercely assaulted by the modern
spirit. Undoubtedly on the points of the ecclesiastical
hierarchy, of man's nature before and after the Fall,
of justification, of the mass, of the invocation of saints
and 'angels, of the worship of images, of purgatory
and many others, we are as unflinchingly opposed to
Rome as our fathers were. But does not current literature show that these are not now the points on which
the struggle of the age is concentrated? Are not the
lines of battle drawn as follows: Theism over against
Pantheism; sin over against imperfection; the divine
Christ of 'God over against Jesus the mere man;
the cross a sacrifice of reconciliation over against
the cross as a symbol of martyrdom; the Bible as
given by inspiration of God over against a purely
human product; the ten commandments as ordained
by God over against a mere archaeological document;
the ordinances of God absolutely established over against
'an ever-changing law and morality spun out of man's
subjective consciousness? Now in this conflict Rome
is not an antagonist, but stands on our side, inasmuch

as she also recognises and maintains the Trinity, the
Deity of Christ, the Cross as an atoning sacrifice, the
Scriptures as the Word of God, and the ten Commandments as a divinely imposed rule of life. Therefore,
let me ask, if Roman theologians take up the sword
to do valiant and skilful battle against the same tendency
that we ourselves mean to fight to the death, is it not
the part of wisdom to accept the valuable help of their
elucidation? Calvin at least was accustomed to appeal
to Thomas of Aquino. And I for my part am not
ashamed to confess that on many points my views
have been clarified through the work of the Romish
students.

This, however, does not in the least involve, that
our hope for the future may be placed in Rome's eu
deavour, and that we, idle ourselves, may await Rome's
victory. A rapid survey of the situation will suffice to
convince us of the contrary. To begin with your own
continent, can South-America for a moment stand a
comparison with the North? Now in South and Central-
America the Roman Catholic Church is supreme. It
has exclusive control in this territory, Protestantism
not even counting as a factor. Here, then, is an immense field in which the social and political power,
which Rome can bring to bear upon the regeneration
of our race, can freely exert itself, a field, moreover,
in which Rome is not a recent arrival, but which she
has occupied for almost three centuries. The youthful
development of the social organism of these countries
has stood under her influence; she has remained in
control also of their intellectual and spiritual life since

their liberation from Spain and Portugal. Moreover the population of these States is derived from
such European countries as have always been under
the undisputed sway of Rome. The test, therefore,
is as complete and fair as possible. But in vain do
we look in those American Romish States for a life
which elevates, develops energy, and exerts a wholesome
influence outside. Financially they are weak, compa-
ratively unprogressive in their economic conditions; in
their political life they present the sad spectacle of
endless internal strife; and, if one were inclined to form
an ideal picture of the future of the world, he might
almost do so by imagining the very opposite of what
is the actual situation in South-America. Nor can it be
pleaded in excuse of Rome that this is due to exceptional circumstances, for in the first place this political
backwardness is met with not only in Chili, but likewise
in Peru, in Brazil as well as in the Venezuelian Republic;
while, crossing from the new to the old world, we reach,
in spite of ourselves, the same conclusion. In Europe,
also, the credit of all Protestant states is high, that of
the Southern' Countries which are Roman Catholic, is
at a painful discount, Economic and administrative
affairs in Spain and Portugal, and not less than in Italy,
offer cause for continual complaint. The outward power
and outside influence of these states is visibly declining.
And, what is more discouraging still, infidelity and a
revolutionary spirit have made such inroads in these
countries, that half of the population, though still
nominally Romish, has in reality broken with all true
religion. This may be seen in France, which is almost

entirely Roman Catholic, and yet has voted time and
again with overwhelming majorites against the advocates
of religion. In fact we may say that, in order to
appreciate the noble, energetic traits of the Romanists,
one must observe them, not in their own countries
where they are on the decline, but in Centrum of Protestant North-Germany, in Protestant Holland and
England, and in your own Protestant States. In regions
where, deprived of a controlling influence, they adjust
themselves to the polity of others and concentrate their
strength as an opposition party, under such leaders as
Manning and Wiseman, Von Ketteler and Windthorst,
they compel our admiration by the enthusiastic championship of their cause.

But even apart from this *testimonium paupertatis* furnished by Rome herself through the mismanagement
in Southern Europe and South-America, where she has
full sway, in the contest of the nations also her power
and influence are visibly waning. The balance of power
in Europe is now gradually passing into the hands of
Russia, Germany and England, every one of them non-
Romish States, and on your own continent the Protestant
North holds the supremacy. Since 1866 Austria has
been continually retrogressing, and at the death of the
present Emperor will be seriously threatened with dissolution. Italy has attempted to live beyond its resources:
it strove to be a great, colonial, naval power, and the
result is that is has brought itself to the verge of economic
ruin. The battle of Addua dealt the death-blow to
more than her colonial aspirations. Spain and Portugal
have absolutely lost all influence on the social, intellec-

tual, and political development of Europe. And France, which only fifty years ago made all Europe tremble at the unsheathing of her sword, is now herself anxiously scanning the Sibylline books of her future. Even from a statistical point of view, the power of Rome is all the while decreasing. Economic and moral depression has in more than one Romish country brought about a considerable decrease of the birthrate. Whilst in Russia, Germany, England and the United States population is growing, it has in some Romish countries become almost stationary. Even now statistics give only the smaller half of Christendom to the Roman-Catholic Church, and it is safe to predict that within the next half century its share will be less than forty per cent. However highly, therefore, I may be inclined to value the inherent power of Roman-Catholic unity and scholarship for the defence of much we also count sacred, and though I do not see how we could repulse the attack of modernism save by combined exertion, nevertheless there is not the slightest prospect that the political supremacy will ever again pass into Rome's hands. And, even if this were to happen contrary to expectations, who could possibly rejoice as in the realization of his ideal, if he beheld the conditions now prevailing in Southern Europe and South America reproduced elsewhere.

We may, in fact, even put it more strongly: it would be a step backwards in the course of history. Rome's world- and life-view represents an older and hence lower stage of development in the history of mankind. Protestantism succeeded it, and hence occupies a

spiritually higher standpoint. He who will not go backwards, but reaches after higher things, must therefore either
stand by the world-view once developed by Protestantism,
or, on the other hand, for this too is conceivable,
point out a still higher standpoint. Now this is
what the latter modern philosophy does indeed presume
to do, acknowledging Luther as a great man for his
time, but hailing in Kant and Darwin the apostles of
a much richer gospel. But this need not detain us. For
our own age, however great in invention, in the display
of powers of mind and energy, has not advanced us a
single step in the establishment of principles, has in no
wise given us a higher view of life, and has yielded us
neither greater stability nor greater soundness in our
religious and ethical i. e. truly human excistence. The
solid faith of the Reformation it has bartered for shift-
ing hypotheses; and in so far as it ventured upon a
systematised and strictly logical life-view it did not
reach forward, but backward, to that Heathen wisdom
of pre-Christian times, of which Paul testified that God
has put it to shame by the foolishness of the Cross. Let
no one therefore say: Ye, who, because history does not
go backward, protest against a return to Rome, ye yourselves have no right to make a stand on Protestantism;
for after Protestantism came Modernism. The perti-
nence of such an objection must be denied, as long as
my contention be not disproved, that the material
advance of our century has nothing in common with
advancement in the matter of ethical principles, and
that what modernism offers us is not modern, but
rather very antique, not posterior, but anterior to

Protestantism, reaching back to the Stoa and to Epicurus.

Only along the lines of Protestantism therefore, can a successful advance be attempted, and on those lines indeed salvation is sought at present, by two different tendencies both of which must lead to bitter disappointment. The one of these is *practical*, the other *mystical* in character. Without hope of defence against modern criticism and still less against criticism of dogma, the former, the practical tendency, holds that Christians can do no better than fall back upon all manner of Christian works. Its devotees are at a loss what attitude to assume towards the Scriptures; they have become themselves estranged from dogma; but what is to prevent such hesitating believers from sacrificing their person and their gold to the cause of philanthropy, evangelism and missions! This even offers a threefold advantage: it unites Christians of all shades of opinion, alleviates much misery, and has a conciliatory attraction for the non-Christian world. And of course this propagandism through action must be gratefully and sympathetically hailed. In the century that has passed, Christian activity was indeed far too limited; and a Christianity that does not prove its worth in practice, degenerates into dry scholasticism and idle talk. It would be a mistake, however, to suppose that Christianity can be confined within the limits of such practical manifestation. Our Saviour made whole the sick and fed the hungry, but the paramount thing in His ministry

17

was, after all, that in strict allegiance to the Scriptures
of the old Covenant, he openly proclaimed His own
Divinity and Mediatorship, the expiation of sins through
His blood, and His coming to judgment. No central
dogma, in fact, has ever been confessed by the church
of Christ which was not the intellectual definition of
what Christ proclaimed about His own mission to the
world, and about the world to which He was sent.
He healed the sick body, but He even more truly
bound up our spiritual wounds. He rescued us from
Paganism and Judaism and translated us into a wholly
new world of convictions of which He Himself as the
God-ordained Messiah constituted the centre. Besides,
so far as our dispute with Rome is concerned, we should
not lose sight of the fact that in Christian works and
devotion Rome still outstrips us. Nay let us acknowledge without reserve that even the unbelieving world
is beginning to rival us, and that in deeds of
philanthropy, she tries more and more to overtake us.
In missions, to be sure, unbelief does not follow in our
footsteps; but pray how can we continue to prosecute
missions, unless we have a well-defined Gospel to preach?
Or is it possible to imagine anything more monstrous
than so called liberal missionaries preaching only humanity and colourless piety, and met by the pagan sages
with the answer that they themselves in their cultured
circles have never taught or believed anything else than
just this modern humanism?

Does perhaps the other tendency, the *mystical* one,
possess stronger powers of defence? What *thinker* or
student of history would affirm this? No doubt mysti-

cism eradiates a fervour that warms the heart; and woe betide the giant of dogma and the hero of action, who are strangers to its depth and tenderness. God created hand, head, and heart, the hand for the deed, the head for the word, the heart for mysticism. King in deed, prophet in profession, and priest in heart, shall man in his threefold office stand before God, and a Christianity that neglects the mystic element grows frigid and congeals. We are therefore to be accounted fortunate whenever a mystic atmosphere envelopes us, making us breathe the balmy air of spring. Through it life is made truer, deeper, and richer. But it would be a sad mistake to suppose that mysticism, taken by itself, can bring about a reversal in the spirit of the age. Not Bernard of Clairvaux but Thomas of Aquino, not Thomas à Kempis but Luther have ruled the spirits of men. Mysticism is, in its very nature, seclusive, and strives rather to avoid contact with the outside world. Its very strength lies in the indifferentiated live of the soul and on this account it cannot take a positive stand. It flows along a subterranean bed and does not show sharply demarcated lines above ground. What is worse, history proves that all one-sided mysticism has always become morbid, and has ultimately degenerated into a mysticism, of the flesh astounding the world with its moral infamy.

Accordingly, although I rejoice in the revival of both the practical and mystical tendencies, both will result in loss instead of gain, if they are expected to compensate for the abandonment of the Truth of Salvation. Mysticism is sweet and Christian works are precious, but the seed of the church, both at the birth of Christianity and in the age of the Reformation has been the blood of martyrs; and our sainted martyrs shed their blood not for mysticism and not for philanthropic projects, but for the sake of convictions such as concerned the acceptance of the truth and the rejection of error. To live with *consciousness* is man's well-nigh divine prerogative, and only from the clear unobscured vision of conscious- . ness proceeds the mighty *word* that can make the times reverse their current, and cause a revolution in the spirit of the world. It is self-deception, therefore, and only self-deception, when these practical and mystical Christians believe they can do without a Christian life and world-view of their own. No one can do without that. Every one who thinks he can abandon the Christian Truths and do away with the Catechism of Reformation, lends ear unawares to the hypotheses of the modern world-view and, without knowing how far he has drifted already, swears by the Catechism of Rousseau and Darwin.

———————

Therefore let us not stop half-way. As truly as every plant has a root, so truly does a principle hide under every manifestation of life. These principles are interconnected and have their common root in a fundamental principle; and from the latter is developed logically and systematically the whole complex of ruling ideas and conceptions that go to make up our life and world-view. With such a coherent world and life-view, firmly resting on its principle and self-consistent in its splendid structure, modernism now confronts Christianity ; and against this deadly danger, ye, Christians, cannot succesfully defend your Sanctuary, but by placing, in opposition to all this, *a life and world-view of your own, founded as firmly on the base of your own principle, wrought out with the same clearness and glittering in an equally logical consistency.* Now this is not obtained by either Christian works or mysticism, but only by going back, our hearts full of mystical warmth and our personal faith manifesting itself in abundant fruit, to that turning-point in history and in the development of humanity which was reached in the Reformation. *And this is equivalent to a return to Calvinism.* There is no choice here. Socinianism died an inglorious death; Anabaptism perished in wild revolutionary orgies. Luther never worked out his fundamental thought. And Protestantism taken in a general sense, without further differentiation, is either a purely negative conception without content, or a chameleon-like name which the deniers of the God-man like to adopt as their shield. Only of Calvinism can it be said that it has consistently and logically followed out the lines of the Reformation, has established not only churches but also States, has set its stamp upon social and public life, and has thus, in the full sense of the world, created for the whole life of man a world of thought entirely its own.

I feel convinced that, after what I have said in my first Lectures, no one will accuse me of underrating Lutheranism; yet the present Emperor of Germany has no less than three times furnished an example of the evil after-effect of Luther's apparently slight mistakes.

Luther was misled into recognizing the Sovereign of
the land as the head of the etablished church, and what
have we as a result of this been called upon to witness
from Germany's eccentric Emperor? First of all that
Stöcker, the champion of Christian democracy, was
dismissed from his court, merely because this bold
defender of the freedom of the churches had so much
as expressed the wish that the Emperor should abdicate
his chief episcopate. Next that, at the sailing of the
German squadron for China, Prince Henry of Russia
was instructed to carry to the far Orient not the
"Christian" but the "*imperial* gospel". More recently
that he called upon his loyal subjects to be faithful in
the performance of their duties, urging as a motive
that after death they were to appear before God....
and His Christ?.... No; but.... before God....
and the great Emperor. And finally on the banquet of
Porta Westphalia, that Germany had to continue its
labours undisturbedly under the blessing of peace, as
enjoined, he concluded, *by the out-stretched hand of
the great Emperor, who here stands above us.* Ever
bolder encroachment, it will be noticed, of Caesarism
upon the essence of the Christian religion. These as
you see, are far from mere trifles; rather they touch
principles of world-wide application, for which our fore-
fathers in the age of the Reformation fought their great
battles. To repristination I am as averse as any man;
but in order to place for the defence of Christianity,
principle over against principle, and world-view over
against world-view, there lies at hand, for him who is
a Protestant in bone and morrow, only *the Calvinistic*

principle as the sole trustworthy foundation on which to build.

What then are we to understand by this return to Calvinism? Do I mean that all believing Protestants should subscribe the sooner the better to the Reformed symbols, and thus all ecclesiastical multiformity be swallowed up in the unity of the Reformed church-organisation? I am far from cherishing so crude, so ignorant, so unhistorical a desire. As a matter of course, there is inherent in every conviction, in every confession, a motive for absolute and unconditional propagandism, and the word of Paul to Agrippa: "I would to God that with little or with much, not you only, but also all that hear me this day, might become such as I am", must remain the heart-felt wish not only of every good Calvinist, but of every one who may glory in a firm immovable conviction. But so ideal a desire of the human heart can never be realized, in this our dispensation. First of all, not one Reformed standard, not even the purest, is infallible as was the word of Paul. Then again the Calvinistic confession is so deeply religious, so highly spiritual, that, excepting always periods of profound religious commotion, it will never be realized by the large masses, but will impress with a sense of its inevitability only a relatively small circle. Furthermore our inborn onesidedness will always necessarily lead to the manifestation of the church of Christ in many forms. And, last not least, absorption on a large scale by one church of the members of another can only take place at critical moments in history. In the ordinary run of things eighty per cent of the Christian population die in the church in which they were born and baptized. Besides, such an identification of my programme with the absorption of one church by another would be at variance with the whole tendency of my argument. Not ecclesiastically, confined to a narrow circle, but as a phenomenon of universal significance, have I commended to you the Calvinism of history. Therefore what I ask, may in the main be reduced to the following four points: that Calvinism shall no longer be ignored where the after-effects of its influence are still manifest; 2. that Calvinism shall again be made a subject of study in order that the outside world may cease to misrepresent it; 3. that its principles shall again be developed in accordance with the needs of our time, and consistently applied not only to Theology, but to every department of life; and 4. that the churches which still lay claim to confessing it, shall cease being ashamed of their own confession.

First then, Calvinism should no longer be ignored where it still exists, but rather be retraced where traces of its historical influence are still manifest. A pointing out in detail, with even some degree of completeness, of the traces that Calvinism has everywhere left behind in social and political, in scientific and æsthetic life, would in itself demand a broader study than could be thought of in the rapid course of a lecture. Allow me therefore, addressing an American audience, to point out a single feature in your own political life. I have already observed in my third lecture how in the preamble

of more than one of your constitutions, while taking a
decidedly democratic view, nevertheless not the atheistic
standpoint of the French revolution, but the Calvinistic
confession of the supreme sovereignty of God, has been
made the foundation, at times even in terms, as I have
pointed out, corresponding literally with the words
of Calvin. Not a trace is to be found among you of
that cynic anti-clericalism which has become identified
with the very essence of the revolutionary democracy,
in France and elsewhere. And when your President
proclaims a national day of thanksgiving or when
the houses of Congress assembled in Washington,
are opened with prayer, it is ever new evidence
that through American democracy there runs even yet
a vein, which, having sprung from the Pilgrim Fathers,
still exerts its power at the present day. Even your
common-school system, inasmuch as it is blessed with
reading of Scripture and opening prayer, points, though
with decreasing distinctness, to like Calvinistic origin.
Similarly in the rise of your university education, springing for the larger part from individual initiative; in
the decentralized and autonomous character of your
local governments; in your strict and yet not nomistic
Sabbath-observance; in the esteem in which woman is
held among you, without falling into the Parisian deific-
ation of her sex; in your sense for domesticity; in the
closeness of your family ties; in your championship of
free speech and in your unlimited regard for freedom
of conscience; in all this your Christian democracy is
in direct opposition to the democracy of the French
revolution; and historically also it is demonstrable that

you owe this to Calvinism and to Calvinism alone. But, lo and behold, while you are thus enjoying the fruits of Calvinism, and while even outside of your borders the constitutional system of government as an out-come of Calvinistic warfare, upholds the national honour, it is whispered abroad that all these are to be accounted blessings of Humanism, and scarcely any one still thinks of honouring in them the after-effect of Calvinism, the latter being believed to lead a lingering life only in a few dogmatically petrified circles. / What I demand then, and demand with an historic right, is that this ungrateful ignoring of Calvinism shall come to an end; that the influence it has exerted shall again receive attention where it still remains stamped upon the actual life of to-day; and that, where men of a wholly different spirit would unobservedly divert the current of life into French-revolutionary or German-pantheistic channels, you on this side of the water, and we on our side, should oppose with might and main such falsification of the historic principles of our life.

That we may be enabled to do so, I contend in the second place for an historical study of the principles of Calvinism. | No love without knowledge; and Calvinism has lost its place in the hearts of the people. It is being advocated only from a theological point of view, and even then very one-sidedly and merely as a side-issue. The cause of this I have pointed out in a previous lecture. Since Calvinism arose, not from an abstract system, but from life itself, it never was in the century of its prime presented as a systematic whole. The tree blossomed and yielded its fruit, but without

any one having made a botanic study of its nature and
growth. Calvinism, in its rise, rather acted than argued.
But now this study may no longer be delayed. Both
the biography and biology of Calvinism must now be
thoroughly investigated and thought out, or, with our
lack of self-knowledge, we shall be side-tracked into a
world of ideas that is more at discord than in consonance
with the life of our Christian democracy, and cut loose
from the root on which we once blossomed so vigorously.

Only through such study will there become possible
what I named in the third place: the development of the
principles of Calvinism in accordance with the needs of
our modern consciousness, and their application to every
department on life. I do not exclude theology from
this; for theology too exercises its influence upon life
in all its ramifications; and it is, therefore, sad to see
how even the theology of the Reformed Churches has
in so many a country come under the sway of wholly
foreign systems. But, at all events, theology is only
one of the many sciences that demand Calvinistic treatment. Philosophy, psychology, æsthetics, jurisprudence, the social sciences, literature, and even the
medical and natural sciences, each and all of these,
when philosophically conceived, go back to principles,
and of necessity even the question must be put with much
more penetrating seriousness than hitherto, whether
the ontological and anthropological principles that reign
supreme in the present method of these sciences are
in agreement with the principles of Calvinism, or are
at variance with their very essence.

Finally I would add to these three demands — historically

justified as it seems to me — still a fourth, that those churches which yet lay claim to professing the Reformed faith, shall cease being ashamed of this confession. You have heard how broad my conception and how wide my views are, even in the matter of ecclesiastical life. In free development only do I see the salvation of this Church-life. I exalt multiformity and hail in it a higher stage of development. Even for the church that has the purest confession, I would not dispense with the aid of other churches in order that its inevitable onesided-ness may thus be complemented. | But what has always filled me with indignation was to behold a church or to meet the office-bearer of a church, with the flag furled or hidden under the garb of office, instead of being thrown out boldly to display its glorious colours in the breeze. What one confesses to be the truth, one must also dare to practise in word, deed and whole manner of life. A church Calvinistic in origin and still recognizable by its Calvinistic confession, which lacks the courage, nay rather which no longer feels the im-pulse to defend that confession boldly and bravely against all the world, such a church dishonours not Calvinism but itself. Albeit the churches reformed in bone and marrow may be small and few in numbers, as churches they will always prove indispensable for Calvinism; and here also the smallness of the seed need not disturb us, if only that seed be sound and whole, instinct with generative and irrepressible life.

And thus my final lecture is rapidly drawing to its

end. But before I close, I feel nevertheless that one
question continues to press for an answer, which accordingly I shall not refuse to face, the question namely,
at what I am aiming in the end: at the abandonment
or at the maintenance of the doctrine of election.
Thereunto allow me to contrast with this word *Election*
another word that differs from it in a single letter.
Our generation turns a deaf ear to *Election*, but grows
madly enthusiastic over *Selection*. How then may we
formulate the tremendos problem that lies hidden behind
these two words, and in what particular do the solutions
of this problem, as represented by these two, almost
identical formules, differ? The problem concerns the
fundamental question: *Whence are the differences?
Why is not all alike?* Whence is it that one thing
exists in one state, another in another? There is no life
without differentiatio n, and no differentiation without
inequality. The perception of difference the very source
of our human consciousness, the causative principle of
all that exists and grows and develops, in short the
mainspring of all life and thought. I am therefore
justified in asserting that in the end every other problem
may be reduced to this one problem : Whence are those
differences? Whence is the dissimilarity, the heterogeneity
of existence, of genesis, of consciousness? To put it
concretely, if you were a plant you would rather be
rose than mushroom; if insect, butterfly rather than
spider; if bird, eagle rather than owl; if a higher verte-
brate, lion rather than hyena; and again, being man,
rich rather than poor, talented rather than dullminded,
of the Aryan race rather than Hottentot or Kaffer.

Between all these there is differentiation, wide differentiation. Everywhere then *differences*, differences between the one being and the other; and that too
such differences as involve in almost every instance,
preference. When the hawk rends and tears the dove,
whence is it that these two creatures are thus opposed to, and different from each other? This is the
one supreme question in the vegetable and animal
kingdom, among men, in all social life, and it is by
means of the theory of *Selection* that our present age
attempts to solve this problem of problems. Even in
the single cell it posits differences, weaker and stronger
elements. The stronger overcomes the weaker, and the
gain is stored up in a higher potency of being. Or,
should the weaker still maintain its subsistence, the
difference will be manifest in the further course of the
struggle itself.

Now the blade of grass is not conscious of this, and
the spider goes on entrapping the fly, the tiger killing
the stag, and in those cases the weaker being does not
account to itself for its misery. But we men are clearly
conscious of these differences, and by us therefore the
question cannot be evaded, whether the theory of
Selection be a solution calculated to reconcile the weaker,
the less richly endowed creature, with its existence. It
will be acknowledged that in itself this theory can but
incite to a more furious struggle, with a *lasciate ogni
speranza, voi che'ntrate* for the weaker being. Against
the ordinance of fate that the weaker shall succumb to
the stronger, according to the system of election, no
struggle can avail. The reconciliation, not springing

from the facts, would therefore have to spring from the *idea*. But what is here the idea? Is it not this, that, where these differences have once become established, and highly differentiated beings appear, this is either the result of chance, or else the necessary consequence of blind natural forces? Now, are we to believe that suffering humanity will ever become reconciled to its suffering by *such* a solution? Nevertheless I welcome the progress of this theory of Selection; and I admire the penetration and power of thought of the men who commend it to us. Not, forsooth, on account of what it urges upon us as a truth; but because it has mustered courage to attack once more the most fundamental of all problems, and thus in point of profundity reaches the same depth of thought, to which Calvin boldly descended.

For this is precisely the high significance of the doctrine of *Election* that, in this dogma, as long as three centuries ago, Calvinism dared to face this same all-dominating problem, solving it, however, not in the sense of a blind selection stirring in unconscious cells, but honouring the sovereign choice of Him Who created all things visible and invisible. The determination of the exis-tence of all things to be created, of what is to be camellia or buttercup, nightingale or crow, hart or swine, and, equally among men, the determination of our own persons, whether one is to be born as girl or boy, rich or poor, dull or clever, white or coloured or even as Abel or Cain, is the most tremendous predesti-nation conceivable in heaven or on earth; and still we see it taking place before our eyes every day, and we

ourselves are subject to it in our entire personality;
our entire existence, our very nature, our position in
life being entirely dependent on it.   This all-embracing
predestination, the Calvinist places, not in the hand
of man, and still less in the hand of a blind natural
force, but in the hand of Almighty God, Sovereign
Creator and Possessor of heaven and earth; and it is
in the figure of the potter and the clay that Scripture
has from the time of the Prophets expounded to us
this all-dominating election.   Election in creation, election in providence, and so election also to eternal life;
election in the realm of *grace* as well as in the realm
of *nature*.   Now, when we compare these two systems
of *Selection* and *Election*, does not history show that
the doctrine of Election has century upon century,
restored peace and reconciliation to the hearts of the
believing sufferer; and that all Christians hold election
as we do, in honour, both in *creation* and in *providence*;
and that Calvinism deviates from the other Christian
confessions in this respect only, that, grasping unity
and placing the glory of God above all thing, it dares
to extend the mystery of Election to spiritual life, and
to the hope for the life to come.

   This then is what Calvinistic dogmatic narrowness
amounts to.   Or rather, for the times are too serious
for irony or jest, lest every Christian, who cannot yet
abandon his objections, at least put this all-important
question to himself: Do I know of another solution of
this fundamental world-problem emabling me better to
defend my Christian faith, in this hour of sharpest
conflict, against renewed Paganism collecting its forces

and gaining day by day? Do not forget that the fundamental contrast has always been, is still, and will be until the end: *Christianity* and *Paganism*, the idols or the living God. So far there is a deeply felt truth in the drastic picture drawn by the German Emperor, representing Buddhism as the coming enemy. A closely drawn curtain hides the future; but Christ has prophesied to us on Patmos the approach of a last and bloody conflict, and even now Japan's gigantic development in less than forty years has filled Europe with fear for what calamity might be in store for us from the cunning "yellow race" forming so large a proportion of the human family. And did not Gordon testify that his Chinese soldiers, with whom he defeated the Taipings, if only well drilled and officered, made the most splendid soldiers he ever commanded? The Asiatic question is in fact of most serious import. The problem of the world took its rise in Asia, and in Asia it will find its final solution; and, both in technical and material development, the issue has shown that heathen nations, as soon as they awake, and arise from their lethargy, rival us almost instantly.

Of course this danger would be far less menacing in case Christendom, in both the old and the new world, stood united around the Cross, shouting songs of praise to their King, and ready as in the days of the days of the crusades to advance to the final conflict. But how when *pagan* thought, *pagan* aspirations, *pagan* ideals are gaining ground even among us and penetrating to the very heart of the rising generation? Have not the Armenians, just because the conception of Christian solidarity has become

so sadly weakened, been basely and cravenly abandoned
to the fate of assassination? Has not the Greek been crushed
by the Turk, while Gladstone, the Christian statesman,
politically a Calvinist to the very core, who had the
courage to brand the Sultan "Great Assassin", has
departed from among us? Accordingly radical determination must be insisted upon. Half-measures cannot
guarantee the desired result. Superficiality will not
brace us for the conflict. Principle must again bear
witness against principle, world-view against world-view,
spirit against spirit. And here, let him who knows
better speak, but I for one know of no stronger and
no firmer bulwark than Calvinism, provided it be taken
in its sound and vigorous formation.

And if you retort, half mockingly, am I really naif
enough to expect from certain Calvinistic studies a
reversal in the Christian world-view, then be the following my answer: The quickening of life comes not
from men: it is the prerogative of God, and it is due to His
sovereign will alone, whether or not the tide of religious life
rise high in one century, and run to a low ebb in the
next. In the moral world, too, we have at one time,
spring, when all is budding and rustling with life, and
again, the cold of winter, when every vital stream
congeals, and all religious energy is petrified.

Now the period in which we are living at present,
is surely at a low ebb religiously.

Unless God send forth His Spirit, there will be
no turn, and fearfully rapid will be the descent of the
waters. But you remember the Aeolian Harp, which
men were wont to place outside their casement, that

the breeze might wake its music into life. Until the wind blew, the harp remained silent, while, again, even though the wind arose, if the harp did not lie in readiness, a rustling of the breeze might be heard, but not a single note of ethereal music delighted the ear. Now, let Calvinism be nothing but such an Aeolian Harp,—absolutely powerless, as it is, without the quickening. spirit of God — still we feel it our God-given duty to keep our harp, its strings tuned aright, ready in the window of God's Holy Sion, awaiting the breath of the Spirit.

www.ingramcontent.com/pod-product-compliance
Lightning Source LLC
Chambersburg PA
CBHW030344270326
41926CB00009B/957